POPULATION ESTIMATES

POPULATION ESTIMATES

METHODS FOR SMALL AREA ANALYSIS

edited by

EVERETT S. LEE
HAROLD F. GOLDSMITH

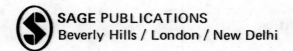

SAGE PUBLICATIONS
Beverly Hills / London / New Delhi

For information address:

SAGE Publications, Inc.
275 South Beverly Drive
Beverly Hills, California 90212

SAGE Publications India Pvt. Ltd.
C-236 Defence Colony
New Delhi 110 024, India

SAGE Publications Ltd
28 Banner Street
London ECIY 8QE, England

Printed in the United States of America

Library of Congress Cataloging in Publication Data

Main entry under title:

Population estimates.

"Results of the Small Area Estimation Conference sponsored by the National Institute of Mental Health (NIMH) and held in Annapolis, Maryland in November, 1978"—Introd.
  Bibliography: p.
  1. Population forecasting—Congresses. I. Lee, Everett Spurgeon. II. Goldsmith, Harold F. III. Small Area Estimation Conference (1978: Annapolis, Md.) IV. National Institute of Mental Health (U.S.)
HB849.53.P66   304.6'2'028   82-648
ISBN 0-8039-1812-7   AACR2

FIRST PRINTING

Contents

Foreword

An important characteristic of a science as it matures is that its measurement becomes more accurate, and the limitations of the measurement procedures become known. In this sense, small area analysis has progressed substantially over the years, and this volume is a tribute to this progress.

A substantial stimulus for the current work comes from the pragmatics of government, the need to know characteristics of small areas in order to allocate resources appropriately according to legislative mandates. However, this thrust conveniently dovetails with important theoretical interests for ecologists, demographers, and other social scientists. If changes occur in communities, presumably they occur for knowable reasons, and these are the bases of theories of change. Charting the change, however, is no simple task, since the basic information source that demographers use is the census, and that source is available only every ten years. In history, a decade may be a short period, but for those dependent on that knowledge as beneficiaries of government policies, a decade is a period almost beyond comprehension. Changes in communities may be slow and incremental, but recent history has seen massive growth in some areas and massive abandonment in other areas. Often the small areas associated with these quick changes are those that are most relevant to those who use the small area data for policy purposes.

Estimates of change can be simple projections on the assumption that the best knowledge of the future is an extension of the past. For some purposes this is enough, but, with regard to

changes in communities, just those other types of changes are
the critical ones to know. While emphasis needs to be put on
what goes into appropriate simple historical projections, the art
of small area analysis moves in the direction of introducing
other sources of information to make the projections meaningful. Attention is required to where these sources can be found
and how they can be tied to the census. It is not an easy process, and a first point that has to be remembered is that error
will always be present if for no other reason than that even the
censuses have error; most other data collection procedures, for
reasons of cost and incompleteness, are going to have more
error. Thus, anticipating the kinds of errors that are going to be
found is important. Knowing the directions of errors involved is
equally important. And estimating the size of errors seems to be
the thing that gives those working in this field some sense of
science.

Even if there were a continuous registration system that
presumably would locate each person in society, there would be
problems in monitoring changes in communities. The ever
present problems are those of costs necessary for the monitoring and maintenance of records, but the costs alone are not
what keep us from having such a system. There are political and
philosophical issues that are critically involved. However, in the
absence of this type of data source, what are the substitutes?
Some of the materials presented in this volume indicate what is
currently done, as in the use of tax records. These provide an
important basis for making estimates of small areas, but they
are not without serious limitations. Survey procedures, the
bread and butter of social science, can also serve as a basis for
estimating change, and some of this approach is covered in this
volume. Then, there are models that fit the patterns of community change based on processes of growth and migration, and
these also receive attention.

No single book can cover all that has been done in small area
analysis, but this book does a great deal in a relatively short
space. Possibly it is so efficient because the field is under
constant surveillance by the population of users, who tend to be

pragmatically oriented legislators and administrators. It is a pressure for validity that may sometimes make for discomfort, but it is also a reasonable test for scientific credibility. Fortunately, this volume displays the fact that social scientists do make progress. What should be even more attractive for the reader is that this volume also communicates something about future developments in estimating small area characteristics.

—Edgar F. Borgatta

Preface

The subject of this monograph, *Population Estimates: Methods for Small Area Analysis,* is how to make better estimates of small (subcounty) area population characteristics. Currently, population estimation is a flourishing business because states have joined the federal government in requiring estimates before allocating funds to local agencies, and because businesses have increased their use of small area estimates in decision making. The environmental statements required for many kinds of construction require detailed estimates. Courts have begun to demand population estimates by race for small areas before permitting the reconstitution of political entities, and juries are frequently challenged as to their representativeness on the basis of current population estimates. Sometimes the needs of business or government can be satisfied by an estimate of total number; more often characteristics such as ethnicity, poverty, income, or household status are required. While estimates for counties and larger areas can be made with acceptable accuracy, it is not yet possible to make similarly accurate estimates for small areas, particularly if it has been a long time since a census. Without careful estimates, we must proceed with important decisions on the basis of the oldest and still most widely used form of estimation, the informed guess.

Because the need for current demographic information is so pressing for health planning and assessment, a conference was arranged by the National Institute of Mental Health to explore some of the newer and more promising small area estimation methods. The papers and critiques that were presented, as well as a summary of the salient points of the discussions that followed, are the subject of this monograph. The chapters of the book provide information about five estimation procedures—administrative records, synthetic surveys, simulation, and area cohorts. The monograph concludes with an essay on the future of small area population estimation.

This monograph provides significant insights into the current state of the art for conducting small area population estimates. It will be of direct interest to demographers and research scientists concerned with developing usable procedures for making small area population estimates, government administrators and business executives who have to make decisions as to the feasibility of doing small area estimates. In addition, the monograph should be of interest to demographers, sociologists, and economists, particularly, those concerned with keeping track of social change.

—Everett S. Lee
—Harold F. Goldsmith

Part One

The Need for Small Area Estimation

1

Overview

Everett S. Lee and Harold F. Goldsmith

This monograph reports the results of The Small Area Estimation Conference sponsored by the National Institute of Mental Health (NIMH) and held in Annapolis, Maryland in November 1978. The conference focused on the problems of estimating the demographic characteristics of small areas. The subject of this monograph and the conference on which it is based was not whether we should make population estimates for small areas, but how we can best make them. Without careful estimates we must proceed with important decisions on the basis of the oldest and still the most widely used form of estimation, the informed guess. The problems before the conference, then, were the ways of improving on current methods and (ways of cutting) the costs involved.

Do we really need to focus on small areas? Why not content ourselves with estimates for regions, states or cities, and assume that variations within these areas will be of small moment? The answer to that question is partly a matter of public policy; federal and state funds are now allocated down to the smallest of places according to population. More important are the roles of place and time in human ecology and epidemiology, in the development of facilities and services, and in the general conduct of government and business.

To the ecologist and epidemiologist, place and time are fundamental considerations, as they are to health service providers and planners. Just as the climatologist stresses the existence of microclimates that differ sharply from each other within a general area and fluctuate with the seasons and environmental changes wrought by man, ecologists and epidemiologists recognize that almost all social pathologies vary greatly from place to place, even from neighborhood to neighborhood. By necessity, a basic unit for analysis and planning is the small area considered at specific times. Students of infectious disease have long been aware of this, but chronic disease, poverty, and intellectual development have only recently been tied to small areas and to the short periods of time over which crucial physical and behavioral developments occur.

One could argue that the census provides all the information needed or likely to be acquired about large numbers of small areas. Unfortunately, that mammoth undertaking occurs only once in ten years, a very long time given the pace of change. In ten years cities can pass from apparent prosperity to outright bankruptcy, and one region may gain primacy over another. Neighborhoods that were stable and attractive may decay as middle-class residents are replaced by poorer people who divide single-family homes into apartments or convert them into rooming houses, while other neighborhoods undergo the contrary process of "gentrification." Areas that were once swamped with migrants may cease to be attractive and begin to lose lifelong residents, while others may become the new Meccas for industry and entertainment. Such is one result of the extraordinary mobility of Americans. From the end of World War II until the recent recession, one in five persons changed place of residence each year, one in fourteen moved from one county to another, and one in thirty moved from one state to another. With mobility of this order it takes little time to effect marked changes in the distribution of population or to redistribute ethnic groups from one area to another.

In actuality, the federal census only occasionally supplies the needed population and housing data. What is wanted is current data; what the census supplies is data for a particular day in the past. Census data are never available on a timely basis. On

January 1, 1981, the Director of the Bureau of the Census delivered to the President the first results of the 1980 Census. These data are based upon the few questions that were asked of all respondents, and they will be revised. More detailed population and housing data become available later, in some cases years after the census. Obviously, what one depends upon the census for is base data upon which to build population estimates. For example, the death rates for the census year, 1980, as announced by the National Center for Health Statistics, will be based upon an estimate of the midyear population, an estimate made necessary by the passage of three months from the date of the census. As time goes on, the estimates are further and further removed from the base date of the census.

Few people are aware that estimating populations for small areas has become a minor industry. The Bureau of the Census regularly makes estimates for over 30,000 areas, and state demographers are charged with preparing population estimates for counties, municipalities, and other small areas. The Atlanta Regional Commission makes estimates for census tracts in its metropolitan area, as do similar agencies elsewhere. In Rochester, N.Y., detailed estimates for each census tract are kept current using complex simulation procedures, and similar programs are under way in other cities. In addition to the official and semiofficial agencies are the firms and individuals who prepare estimates for business and government.

Currently, population estimation is a flourishing business because states have joined the federal government in requiring estimates before allocating funds to local agencies, and because businesses have increased their use of small area estimates in decision making. The environmental statements needed for many kinds of construction require detailed estimates. For example, before atomic plants are constructed it may be necessary to estimate the population within circles of one, two, three, four, and five miles around the plant, and then by five or ten mile steps up to seventy miles, all by 22.5 degree segments. Courts have begun demanding population estimates by race for small areas before permitting the reconstitution of political

entities, and juries are frequently challenged as to their representativeness on the basis of current estimates. Sometimes the
needs of business or government can be satisfied by an estimate
of total number; more often characteristics such as ethnicity,
poverty, income, or household status are required. It is not
simple to make such estimates for small areas, particularly if it
has been a long time since a census. Because the need for
current demographic information is so pressing for health
planning and assessment, the Small Area Estimation Conference
was arranged by the Mental Health Study Center of the
National Institute of Mental Health to explore some of the
newer and more promising methods. The papers that were
presented and a summary of the discussions that followed are
the subject of this monograph. The order of presentation is
given below along with a brief statement of the subject of each
session.

ORDER OF PRESENTATION

DEDICATION TO C. HORACE HAMILTON

The conference was dedicated to C. Horace Hamilton. More
than any other person, Hamilton made the improvement of
population estimates an overriding concern. He dealt with the
improvement of death and birth reporting and allocation, but
above all, he focused upon the most difficult part of the
estimation process, the assessment of migration. His was a major
role in developing procedures of estimating migration with
survival techniques, and with Jacob Siegel of the Bureau of the
Census, he wrote the classic paper, "Use of the Survival Rate
Method in Measuring Net Migration" (Hamilton and Siegel,
1944). While others were still reluctant to estimate state populations, Hamilton was already preparing estimates of populations
for counties, and when others spoke in general about the effects
of migration on the South, Hamilton was busy estimating the

net flows by race and education. His interests were more than theoretical. He became in effect the state demographer for North Carolina, and tested his methods by preparing the estimations that the state used in allocating budgets and constructing facilities. As Gladys Bowles sets out in Appendix A, Hamilton was the rare person who switches easily from pragmatic undertakings to abstract methodological inquiries.

TONE OF THE CONFERENCE

In opening the conference, Everett Lee drew upon Hamilton's experiences to emphasize the continuing need for attempts to do what so many people declare as impossible. He noted that when the Census Bureau was called upon to make its first series of estimates for the United States, there were those who declared it impossible. And when state estimates were demanded, the chorus of doubters grew louder still. Finally, when the Bureau of the Census was forced by Congressional action to prepare estimates for thousands of small areas, there was great concern. Nevertheless, it was done, and, in the light of available evidence, it was done well. Error, of course, is impossible to avoid, and for small areas the percentage error may seem staggering even when the absolute error is unimportant.

DISCUSSIONS OF PRESENTATIONS

The major papers presented at the conference were prepared and distributed prior to the conference (see list of participants in this volume). The discussion that followed a short presentation of each major paper was led by a discussant who had studied the paper beforehand. His remarks, which may have been somewhat modified at the session, follow each major paper in the monograph along with a synopsis of the open discussion which followed. Fittingly, the first methodological paper of the conference dealt with the experiences of the

Bureau of the Census in performing the unwelcome but reward-
ing task of preparing estimates for political entities, some so
small they had to be searched for on large-scale maps.

USE OF ADMINISTRATIVE RECORDS IN
MAKING SMALL AREA ESTIMATES

The first presentation in the conference and the first
methodological paper in the monograph, by Mary Kay Healy,
presents the administrative records procedures used by the
Bureau of the Census to estimate net migration for subcounty
areas. This is followed by Donald K. Pittenger's critical examination of administrative record procedures for estimating small
area population characteristics. Both federal and state governments maintain a wide variety of administrative records that can
be used to estimate population and other types of change.
Among the most important of these are the records of the
Internal Revenue Service, which each year receives tax forms
from some 90 million taxpayers. Since these include some
information from the previous year, they are useful in assessing
the mobility of population and, together with other materials,
have made it possible to meet the Congressional demand for
population estimates for subcounty areas. Healy describes the
ways in which these records are used in making estimates for
more than 30,000 places, many of which are small and some of
which have no more than 50 people. This is a task of stu-
pendous proportions and one that depends for its success upon
federal-state cooperation.

The estimates made by the Bureau of the Census are of great
value to business and government, and they are widely used for
purposes other than the allocation of federal and state funds.
For many purposes, however, they are not timely enough and
they are not made for the areas which are of immediate concern
to investors or planners. In many cases data are wanted for areas
that are not defined by political boundaries and must be shaped
according to a market or service district. Fortunately, there are
techniques of using the available data for larger or neighboring

areas to estimate population or population characteristics for smaller or differently defined areas.

SYNTHETIC PROCEDURES

In the second methodological presentation, Peter Francese discusses synthetic procedures for making such estimates. Admittedly, these are desperation techniques, indirect approaches to be used whenever directly relevant information is not available for particular areas or population components. For example, intercensal population estimates may be available for counties, but not for the included municipalities or subdivisions. However, if the desired information is available from the past census for a county and its subdivisions, it is possible to estimate current population characteristics for the subdivisions by making use of ratios computed for the county and its subdivisions at the time of the census. This is an established technique, widely used in business and now undergoing experimentation by governmental bureaus, that is certainly much better than unsystematic extrapolations or uncontrolled surveys. But while admiring the ingenuity of the designers and recognizing the value of the results, one recalls Conant's definition of science as doing one's damnedest with the materials and tools available (Conant, 1951).

SURVEY METHOD

A third approach, the survey method, is more direct. Norfleet W. Rives, Jr. describes a method that involves taking a survey at about the time of the census, relating the findings to the census results, and making a similar survey whenever estimates are wanted. The relationships between the census and the accompanying survey are then used with the following survey to estimate the population and its characteristics at the later time. In his evaluation of the survey approach to small area estimation that follows the paper by Rives, Peter K. Morrison discusses different approaches to monitoring local demographic change.

SIMULATION PROCEDURES

In some ways, the most promising method—the Community Analysis Model—is described by David L. Birch and critically evaluated by Peter Francese. This Community Analysis Model is based upon estimates of behavior by individuals and permits modification of behavior patterns as situations change. Given a particular situation, people act in statistically predictable ways, and in a given area at a given time only so many options are possible. The model is perhaps the most elaborate yet attempted, but it is based upon data that are widely available. Furthermore, its implementation is not beyond the resources of state or city planning agencies. More important, the model has undergone extensive tests, and in the judgment of officials in cities where it has been installed, it works. Now operating in several cities and the State of North Carolina, it will undergo a crucial evaluation when the 1980 Census data become available.

THE AREA COHORT APPROACH

The final methodological paper by Harold F. Goldsmith, David J. Jackson, and J. Philip Shambaugh describes a social area analysis approach to small area estimation. By and large, the estimation of population in small areas is carried out with little regard to differences in the way people live, in the kinds of dwelling units they inhabit, and in the types of households they form. However, tracts or other areas identifiable in the census can be classified by income levels, proportion in poverty, education, occupational group, and many other demographic, social, and economic indicators as well. Furthermore, these indicators may be combined to yield such categorizations as early childrearing, middle childrearing, late childrearing and childlaunching, and post childrearing. Goldsmith and his associates have developed these indicators for all identifiable areas in the 1970 Census and will repeat that task with the 1980 Census. The items in the Mental Health Demographic Profile System that are used to classify small areas are available on tape (see Goldsmith et al., 1981). Reasoning that similar types of social areas experience similar rates of change, the authors show that estimates for census tracts classified by social areas are significantly better than those made for unclassified tracts.

REFERENCES

CONANT, J. B. (1951) Science and Common Sense. New Haven: Yale University Press.

HAMILTON, C. H. and F. M. HENDERSON (1944) "Use of the survival rate method in measuring net migration." Journal of the American Statistical Association 39 (June): 197-206.

GOLDSMITH, H. F., A. S. LEE, and B. M. ROSEN (1982) Small Area Social Indicators. National Institute of Mental Health, Series BN No. 3, DHHS Publication (ADM)82-1189. Washington, DC: Government Printing Office.

Part Two

Using Administrative Records

2

Introduction and Basic Procedures

Mary Kay Healy

At the subcounty level, the Bureau of the Census produces population estimates for incorporated places and minor civil divisions (MCDs) where these exist as townships and towns, and includes both dependent and independent cities incorporated within MCD boundaries. No estimates are currently made for other minor civil division or census county division categories such as precincts and election districts, or for smaller residential areas such as census tracts.

This chapter will outline and illustrate the "administrative records" procedures used by the Bureau to make these estimates. Problems associated with this procedure will be discussed. The Bureau uses a *component technique* whereby the various elements of population change, fertility, mortality and migration, are estimated separately. (For a precise statement of the relationship see equation 1 in Appendix 2.1.) For approximately *one-half of the 39,000* localities estimated, resident vital statistics, birthrate and death rate, are obtained from either the state health departments or the National Center for Health Statistics. For the remaining half, births and deaths are estimated on the basis of national fertility and mortality rates. Special populations, however, are handled individually. Data on immigrants from abroad, college enrollments, military barracks populations, and persons residing in hospitals for long-term treatment and in penal institutions are used to measure the absolute change in these special groups. This information is gathered from the Immigration and Naturalization Service, as well as the various colleges, institutions, and military bases.

The final component—internal migration—is established through the use of federal income tax returns. Basically, the geographic locations from which returns are filed for two different years are matched by social security number. This determines the mover/nonmover status of persons filing income tax returns. The data are taken from questions on the Internal Revenue Service (IRS) forms requesting residence information. The information provided includes incorporated place, township, county and state. The responses obtained from these returns form the basis for a geographic coding guide. The guide used for the 1973 and 1975 subcounty estimates was developed from a 70 percent complete response rate; the current guide is based on information that is complete on 95 percent of all returns filed.

The guides enable one to determine the geographical location of persons who file. The number of exemptions claimed on the matched returns (excluding exemptions for age and blindness) provide the gross migration figures that are used in the computation of specific migration rates for localities. Rates are computed in lieu of using the actual IRS data, since there are unmatched returns, as well as residents who do not file tax returns. This migration rate is applied to the base nongroup quarters population on the assumption that persons not covered by the matched IRS returns migrate in the same patterns as the matched population. Appendix 2.1 outlines in a step-by-step fashion the July 1, 1976 administrative records estimating procedure for Chicago Heights, Illinois. It should be noted that an adjustment factor is used to control all subcounty places to an independent estimate at the next higher level of geography.

EVALUATION OF MCD ESTIMATES

In order to determine whether or not the assumption that persons not covered by the matched IRS returns migrate in the same pattern as matched persons is justified, the number of exemptions on matched returns is tested to determine whether or not these data are sufficiently representative of a specific locality's population. With this information, a coverage ratio—the ratio of the number of exemptions on matched returns to the nongroup quarters base year population—is derived. If this coverage ratio fails set tolerance levels established by the Bureau, the place migration rate is replaced by its respective county migration rate.

There are numerous reasons for poor coverage. Among these are post office consolidations, new incorporations, and places split between different geographic units. In addition, annexations can play havoc with determination of a filer's proper geographic location. Significantly, the smaller the population of the area for which estimates are being prepared, the greater geographical and related problems become.

The most extreme examples of these problems arise in states where MCDs exist, and incorporated places within the various township (MCD) boundaries can be either dependent or independent of the township, or worse, split among several townships.

To provide a better understanding of the problems associated with the census administrative record procedures, Homewood and Hoffman Estates, two places in Cook County, Illinois, that had federally conducted special censuses since 1970 will be examined. Since independent estimates from the special census existed for these localities, a good test of the administrative records estimates is provided. The village of Homewood is split among four townships. The 1970 Census counts for these places were 10,081; 1,259; 1,356; and 6,175 (see Table 2.1). A comparison of the August 8, 1973 special census results interpolated to July 1, 1973 with the respective estimate discloses that for the total village the estimate of 19,362 was 3.4 percent lower than the adjusted special census figure of 20,044. However, the percentage differences for the individual pieces were 6.1, -46.1, -20.0, and 2.4 percent, respectively.

The problems in Homewood appear to be related to the geographic coding of returns. Table 2.1 presents the coverage

TABLE 2.1   Population and Coverage Ratios for the Component Parts
of Homewood, Illinois: 1970 to 1976

Township	Population 1970	Coverage Ratios[1] 1973	1975	1976
Bremen	10,081	98.28	97.98	108.14
Bloom	1,259	163.46	166.15	84.08
Rich	1,356	135.66	137.72	122.97
Thornton	6,175	88.02	92.04	103.53

[1] A Coverage Ratio is the ratio of the number of exemptions on matched returns to the nongroup quarters base year population.

ratios for the three estimate years by split piece. In Homewood, despite poor coverage for its component parts, the migration rates were not unreasonable and were used in the production of the estimates. This is not always the case. For example, in Hoffman Estates, some migration estimates could not be used. The reason for this is clear when one examines the coverage ratios in Table 2.2. Examination of the coverage ratios presented in Table 2.2 reveals high and low coverage ratios for each estimation period. This table of the unadjusted data reveals the problems and inaccuracies involved with the geographic coding of administrative records to small areas. In the actual production of estimates for these areas several of the migration rates were replaced by county migration rates.

Other problems occur in places that may not be split, but are incorporated and dependent within a township. In these situations, most filers tend to list the city as their place of residence rather than the township, causing high coverage ratios in the cities, while the balances of the township are low. As a consequence again, the migration data are usually distorted. Table 2.3 depicts this situation in Ramsey Village and Ramsey Township in Fayette County, Illinois. Even though the migration rates presented in Table 2.3 do not appear implausible, the fact that they switch direction throughout the estimate period generates serious questions as to their validity.

TABLE 2.2   Population, Coverage Ratios, and Migration Rates for the Component Parts of Hofmann Estates, Illinois: 1970 to 1976

Township	Census Population 1970	Coverage Ratios[1] 1973	1975	1976	Migration Rates[2] 1973	1975	1976
Barrington	6	0	0	38.50	0	0	23.38
Hanover	52	278.85	285.71	65.52	24.14	6.43	10.53
Palatine	815	257.55	360.55	107.00	30.92	5.43	−17.01
Schaumberg	21,365	87.79	94.18	97.19	28.01	1.16	2.18

[1] A Coverage Ratio is the ratio of the number of exemptions on matched returns to the nongroup quarters base year population.
[2] Unadjusted for coverage problems.

TABLE 2.3   Population, Coverage Ratios, and Migration Rates for the Component Parts of Ramsey Township, Illinois: 1970 to 1976

Township	Census Population 1970	Coverage Ratios[1]			Migration Rates		
		1973	1975	1976	1973	1975	1976
Ramsey Village	830	103.13	103.36	105.40	− 6.78	2.12	− 1.71
Ramsey Township Balance	1,069	55.00	67.37	88.68	16.33	− 2.29	− 3.51

[1] A Coverage Ratio is the ratio of the number of exemptions on matched returns to the nongroup quarters base year population.

Despite the problems involved with the development of small area population estimates, tests have shown them to fare relatively well from a technical standpoint. As expected, the smaller the area being estimated, the larger the resulting error. The question, then, is whether or not government funding programs are equitable when determined on the basis of population estimates, considering the error levels illustrated in Table 2.4.

PROVIDING ESTIMATES FOR SMALL AREAS— CENSUS TRACTS

Although the cases presented are selected to exhibit potential difficulties of an administrative records approach, such illustrations point up clearly the various problems encountered in the coding and estimating of small areas. These would be intensified if population estimates produced by a component methodology were attempted for census tracts. For such areas, with an average population of about 4000, the figures would probably become meaningless.

In order to code any administrative records file to tract levels, a coding guide such as the Census Bureau's GBF/DIME system would be necessary (U.S. Bureau of the Census, 1976). Currently, GBF/DIME files do not exist for all metropolitan areas, and several of the files in existence have not been updated since 1970. After 1980, these files will have coverage for approximately 65 percent of the U.S. population; however, this will still not be sufficient for data coding in areas that have zip codes, street names, and house changes. In order to resolve these cases and update the GBF system, a massive clerical operation would become necessary. In addition, tract updating for the next census would take place at various times for differing metropolitan areas. In cities that have already revised their GBF, the 1970 base data are still in terms of 1970 tracts, making comparability extremely difficult.

TABLE 2.4 Comparison of 1975 Administrative Records Method Estimates with the Results of Special Censuses Conducted between July 1, 1974 and July 1, 1976, for Subcounty Areas by Size of Area

	All Places	Size of Place (in 1970)				
		50-999	1,000–4,999	5,000–9,999	10,000–49,999	50,000 or more
Number of Places	1,986.0	621.0	636.0	251.0	378.0	100.0
Average Percentage Difference (disregarding sign)	10.7	18.0	9.3	7.0	4.1	3.2

Other problems would be involved with the percentage of administrative record sets that have nonresidence addresses listed, such as a bank or office. This proportion probably varies by file and by area. Also, small areas do not necessarily conform to place boundaries, either in 1970 or currently, because of geography changes such as annexations. The massive annexing program that occurred in Houston is a good case in point since these actions entailed the annexing of numerous partial tracts.

Based on the Census Bureau's experiences in the development of MCD and place estimates, as well as the obvious problems that would occur at the tract level, the production of reliable and timely census tract estimates through the use of administrative records appears unfeasible at this time or in the near future.

REFERENCE

U.S. Bureau of the Census (1976) Documentation for the Geographic Base (DIME) System (GEO-202), January 1, 1973, 3rd Rev. Washington, DC: Government Printing Office.

APPENDIX 2.1: Computation of Population Estimates for Chicago Heights, Illinois

I. Estimation Equation

$$
\begin{aligned}
&\text{July 1, 1976} \\
&\text{Current} \quad = \quad \begin{bmatrix} \text{Last} + \text{Births} - \text{Deaths} + \text{Change in} + \\ \text{Count} \qquad\qquad\qquad\qquad \text{Institutions} \\ \qquad\qquad\qquad\qquad\qquad \text{and Colleges}^1 \\[6pt] \text{Change in} + \text{Immigration} + \text{Nongroup} \\ \text{Military} \qquad \text{from Abroad}^3 \quad \text{Quarters} \\ \text{Barracks} \qquad\qquad\qquad \text{Net Migra-} \\ \text{Population}^2 \qquad\qquad\qquad \text{tion} \end{bmatrix} \times \begin{matrix} \text{Adjustment} \\ \text{to County} \\ \text{Control} \end{matrix} \\
&\text{Estimate}
\end{aligned}
$$

II. Data for Chicago Heights, Illinois

A. Exemptions filed on tax returns in:

	1970	43,993
	1975	40,835
	1976	39,499

B. Exemptions/total population ratio in   1970   107.56

C. Derivation of net migration:

	1975 Population Base	1975-1976
(1) Inmigrants on matched returns		3,183
(2) Outmigrants on matched returns		3,618
(3) Nonmovers on matched returns		34,056
(4) Net migrants on returns (4) = (1) − (2)		−435
(5) Net migration rate for tax returns (5) = 4/[(2) + (3)]		−.01155
(6) Net migration for total population (6) = (5) × (15)		−459

D. Derivation of migration base:

(7) Base population	39,527	
(8) Period resident births		709
(9) Period resident deaths		328
(10) Period natural increase (10) = (8) − (9)		381
(11) Institutional and college population[1] on base date	0	
(12) Military in barracks on base date	0	
(13) Period immigrants from abroad[3]	90	
(14) Nongroup quarters population on base date (14) = (7) − (11) − (12)	39,527	
(15) Nongroup quarters net migration base (15) = (14) = 1/2[(10) + (13)]		39,763

E. Derivation of population estimates:

(16) Institutional and college
population[1] on estimate date   0
(17) Military in barracks on
estimate date[2]   0
(18) Resident population estimate
(18) = (14) + (10) + (13) + (6) +
(16) + (17)   39,539
(19) Adjustment factor to control
country total   .99115
(20) Population estimate
(20) = (18) × (19)   39,189

III. Estimation of Migration Rate

Equation = Equation I with numbers from Part II substituted.

$$(20) = [(7) + (8) - (9) + [(16) - (11)] + [(17) - (12)] + (13) + (6) \times (19)]$$

1976   39,189 = [39,526 + 709 + 328 + (0 - 0) + (0 - 0) + 90 + (-459) × (.99115)]

[1] Only applicable where such populations constitute at least 500 persons and at least 2 percent of the area's total resident population.
[2] Only applicable to military installations with barracks populations of 100 or more.
[3] Based on intended place of residence data from the Immigration and Naturalization Service.

3

Critique of Administrative
Records Procedures

Donald B. Pittenger

The original assignment to this writer was to comment on the chapter by Mary Kay Healy. It is an example of a relatively inexpensive procedure for providing population estimates—the administrative records procedure. Her essay requires little comment because it clearly presents the limitations of using Internal Revenue Service data for estimating total populations for small units. Therefore, I think it would be useful to present a framework for evaluating the administrative records procedures as well as the other techniques presented at the conference. My perspective is that of a technician who also has some government administrative responsibilities.

Ms. Healy is pessimistic about extending "administrative records" population estimation techniques to small areas such as census tracts. Her illustrations of Internal Revenue Service (IRS) record coverage of villages split by township boundaries give cause for concern. Actually, she could have told a more upsetting tale by going into greater detail on reasons for poor coverage. She could have mentioned households living in the country whose address is a post office box in town, and consequently assigned to the wrong residential area. She also might have noted the problem created by persons not filing IRS returns—tests using California county census data suggest that central city residents are less likely to file than suburban residents; therefore, central cities are underestimated and suburbs are overestimated when IRS data are used.

I accept Ms. Healy's argument, so far as it goes. Clearly, the estimation technique she describes may yield estimates of questionable validity for many minor civil divisions or townships, and its extension to areas of even finer geographical detail such as census tracts would be likely to generate worthless data. However, I find her perspective limited. There are more administrative records than those from federal income tax returns, and these can be effectively used to provide good small area population estimates.

One strategy is to use a variety of public records—singly or in combination—to build up a battery of estimation models. A practical approach to the effective use of such data would be to inventory existing public records and see what could be done with them. The Census Bureau's cooperative estimation program does this to some extent, but to date there has been no record matching between data types. While this may entail some additional cost, the cost may not be prohibitive when the value of the data is properly perceived. A discussion of some other types of administrative records that may be used is presented below.

If good records on housing units by type of structure can be created and maintained, the possibility of using a sophisticated version of the housing unit method of population estimation can be used as a check on the IRS procedure, and as an independent method for estimating the characteristics of sub-county geographical units. It is possible to get fairly accurate estimates of population totals using well-designed versions of the housing unit method. This has been done in Washington state. Fundamental to the housing unit method is an accurate inventory of housing stock by type of structure. Unfortunately, such inventories are not yet common. The problem is inventory maintenance. Much change in housing stock is reported through construction or demolition permits, and these data are misleading because issuance of a permit does not mean that construction or demolition will actually occur. Data on conversion of units to different types of structure are often nonexistent. An ideal system would entail tracking of all permits to completion as well as geocoding the location of each housing unit.

Given an accurate data base, vacancy rates and household size by structure type can be obtained by a combination of local censuses, sample surveys, and "windshield" vacancy checks where an observer bias is calibrated against census data. The Washington state estimation system has all these features save the ideal housing stock inventory just described. This approach to population estimation would require funds for inventory maintenance and field operations, but the cost would not be too great. I estimate that nationwide noncensus, nonsurvey field operations could operate for about $10 million per year. Census and survey operations could double or triple the cost. I have no estimate for housing stock inventory and maintenance cost.

A properly done housing unit estimate could be used in conjunction with the IRS method described by Ms. Healy, and the results of the methods could be averaged. Also, other methods could be included. A common method is the use of regression procedures to model changing subarea populations. The extension of this procedure to small areas requires small area administrative records of population-related data. While few such data series exist, there are some candidates for development. Drivers' licenses could be utilized. These records usually contain age and sex characteristics and an address that would permit geocoding. One problem with license data is that changes of address between renewal dates are not always reported. Another problem is that college students and military personnel are very likely to have addresses other than their place of usual residence as defined by the Census Bureau. Adjustment of known changes in college enrollment and military station strength could be used in the regression equations to counteract this problem. An accurate geocoded housing stock inventory—as described above—could also be used in a regression model. Ideally, housing stock should be classified by structure type and perhaps rough household size weights might be introduced. In addition, the geocoding of IRS address data might yield data on claimed exemptions that could be useful in their own right as well as in a regression model. For example, income data could be calculated for very small areas. Bridging such an IRS file to the master Social Security file would yield age-sex-race information on most earners.

One solution entails the "ultimate" administrative record— the population register. If all citizens were registered, as they are in some European countries, and if residence were GBF/ DIME coded and social security numbers linked people to IRS and other data, continuous small area profiles rich in demographic and economic detail could be maintained at comparatively low cost. This is probably the "best" approach from all standpoints save one—the risk of privacy violation.

4

Evaluation and Synopsis

The Editors

OVERVIEW

Whether one is elated by the progress that has been made or depressed by the problems encountered in preparing estimates for small areas depends upon the client to be served and the need for accuracy. When the client is a state or local government, the estimates will almost certainly meet with objections if they do not fit with official preconceptions. In general, local officials are disturbed by evidence of falling population or slowing growth, and prefer larger rather than smaller estimates. It is often difficult for local residents to accept the reality of slow growth or actual decline of population, especially if utility hookups are increasing and areas of settlement are expanding. Both local officials and estimators of national populations have been misled by the greater increase in households than in people that has occurred in the last two decades.

The concern of local officials is heightened by regulations that allocate federal and state funds to localities on the basis of population. Such funds have become an important part of the revenues of towns and cities, sometimes a major part. Those who make official estimates must therefore expect to have them questioned, and we shall see increasing challenges in the courts. But even if no monies were allocated from one governmental level to another, population estimates would remain a serious concern for local officials. In general, growth is equated with progress and it is a matter of pride for many that their community is growing. On the other hand, evidence of lagging growth may be translated into reduced attraction to new businesses and into falling or stagnant real estate values. In short, population estimates assume a dollar and cents value and are an important determiner of the image that outsiders hold of an area.

Though population estimators are much troubled by protests from localities, the long-run effect is to improve the estimates. Local officials do more than challenge faulty estimates; they cooperate in correcting them. Furthermore, it is pressure from the communities that are affected by the estimates that will bring about better data and the research needed to improve procedures.

Local officials will also learn that they can, and must, tolerate some margin of error, even a considerable error as measured on a percentage basis. If, for example, the true population of Loving County, Texas is 50, little is lost for most endeavors if the population is estimated at 75, a 50 percent error; or 25, a contrary error of 50 percent. Of course, that kind of percentage error would not be tolerable for a city of 10,000, though an absolute error of 200 or even of 1,000 might be of little significance. Of course, an error of 1,000 might lead to the overbuilding or underbuilding of facilities, but those who plan for essential services should leave a margin for uncertainty. A relatively small error in population estimates is seldom of much consequence, and planners should be taught to work with uncertainty in mind. Like bridge builders, they must leave a margin for overload.

We tend to ask for too much in the way of accuracy. If we want to be certain of a population, we should take a complete census, as localities do. But that kind of accuracy (and not even the most careful census of a large area can be completely accurate) is achieved at considerable cost. The purpose of estimates is to provide a reasonably accurate figure at the lowest possible cost, and we must always balance the desire for certainty against the cost involved. Even if we take a census, we cannot expect absolute accuracy. All population counts or estimates should be accompanied by estimates of undercount or variation. The Census Bureau attempts this in the decennial censuses when it tries to measure the undercount, and in the Current Population Surveys where monographs are presented against which the published figures may be matched for expected variation.

In a sense, the data presented by Healy do give a measure of the validity of the estimates for small areas. After the somewhat discouraging discussion that preceded, she presents in Table 2.4 a comparison of the 1975 estimates prepared by her office with special censuses conducted between July 1, 1974 and July 1, 1976 for almost 2000 places. As one would expect, the percentage error is greatest for the smallest places and is relatively small for the largest. In fact, a curve drawn through the percentage error by size of place is quite smooth, descending sharply from 18 percent for places of 50 to 1,000 population to 9 percent for the next size class, 1,000-5,000, and then gradually to little more than 3 percent for places of 50,000 or more. Though there are only five points to determine a curve, it does suggest that a fuller comparison of estimates with the 1980 Census would lead to acceptable measures of the variation to be expected with estimates for places of a given size.

At any rate, an error of 18 percent for very small places is tolerable for most purposes and an error of 9 percent for places of 1000 to 5000, a range in which most census tracts are found, is not too distressing. For the larger places, the error is about that which is found when censuses are compared with other data. Admittedly, we know nothing from this article about the distribution around the mean of the errors presented, but these figures are encouraging rather than discouraging. They lead us to surmise that estimates can be prepared by the administrative records method, even at the current stage of development, that are acceptable and that we can eventually accompany these estimates with statements of expected variation.

It is worth making one other point in this regard. Whereas estimates for a single small area may be very much off as measured in terms of percentage error, it is likely that better estimates can be obtained for the combination of small areas that include the one in question. Very often that is exactly what is needed, a reasonable idea of the population of the larger area in which the particular area is included.

Though the discussants were generally more enthusiastic about the quality of the estimates than Healy or others who must explain their estimates to local officials allow themselves to be, it was recognized that there are major problems with the use of administrative records to estimate populations for the years following a census. Among those which must be taken into account are the following:

(1) accuracy of the preceding census
(2) boundary problems: shifts in political or census unit boundaries
(3) residency problems: relationships of areas for which estimates are to be made to those identified in census and administrative records
(4) coverage problems: determination of the degree to which administrative records are representative of the entire population
(5) use of administrative records other than those of the Internal Revenue Service in population estimation
(6) need for local cooperation

ACCURACY OF PRECEDING CENSUS

We should not forget that most types of population estimates are based upon the preceding census; in this sense they may be viewed as projections. Furthermore, adjustments for under- or overcounts depend upon matching census records with administrative records. Obviously, in areas where census records are quite accurate, we can make better estimates than where they are poor. For this reason alone we can be more confident of estimates for stable, white, middle-class areas than we can for areas where there is a large transient population, especially if the population is predominantly black and disproportionately composed of young males or broken families. In the 1970 Census the overall estimate of undercount was about 3 percent.

While it was somewhat less for whites, it approached 10 percent for blacks and 20 percent for black males between the ages of 16 and 25. Consequently, estimates are sometimes better than the census counts, but that is an unlikely possibility. With an administrative records method, we are tied to the preceding census. In general, where the census is good we may expect estimates to be good; unfortunately, the reverse holds even more strongly.

BOUNDARY PROBLEMS

The boundaries of census areas, large or small, do not remain the same over time. Areas are subtracted from one entity and added to another with great regularity. Some places disappear when they are incorporated into another, while others are split and appear as separate entities. This is an especially acute problem with census tracts, which by necessity must undergo some change from time to time. Without current knowledge of annexations and mergers it is easy to be misled and even to impute growth or decline where the opposite has taken place.

RESIDENCY PROBLEMS

Census results are published for politically defined areas and for areas that are defined by the Bureau of the Census as relatively homogeneous, useful for the assignment of enumerators, or for a variety of other reasons, one of which is the necessity of exhausting the area of a state or county to attain full coverage. For the purposes of the census and for political reasons, these are useful areas that both politicians and census officials will defend. Though not ideal, they are sufficient for the administrative necessities of state and local governments and for the Bureau of the Census.

With respect to any area, political or administrative, one of the surprising findings in the study of population estimation is that people do not always know where they live. Their mental image may be different from reality. Of course, they know their state of residence and they usually know their county, especially if they pay property taxes or buy their automobile licenses through county offices, but a great many have no idea as to their township or minor civil division. Certainly, there is no reason for them to know what their census defined division or census tract is. Of course, most people know their post office address, including the zip code, but post office address and residential address are often different.

This is unfortunate for our purposes because we must obtain the location of residence in IRS returns from the zip codes or post office designations. Zip codes and post office designations are assigned by the Post Office Department to facilitate the delivery of mail, and the Post Office has little concern for the political or census subdivisions which are included in or across these boundaries. A zip code or a post office designation may cover a large territory, including several entire census tracts and parts of others, or it may represent a large business or a university. In fact, a zip code may be assigned to a single person. Many people live in one area, but get their mail in another, perhaps through a post office box in a location more convenient to the place of work than near the place of residence. Furthermore, the Post Office Department is about to change its system of zip codes, increasing the number of digits from five to nine, a change that may facilitate the delivery of mail without making it any easier to relate mail addresses to actual residential locations. Just as the Post Office Department has little interest in residential location, except where it affects the delivery of mail, the Internal Revenue Service has little interest except where it affects the collection of taxes.

This is a situation we must live with. While there are dreams of assigning latitude and longitude designations to every dwelling unit, we must in the foreseeable future content ourselves with the development of better ways of relating mail addresses to census tracts or other area units. If an exact address is provided it could be geocoded to a specified subcounty unit, minor civil division, or census tract. Geographic coding guides have been expanded to cover 95 percent of IRS returns; unfortunately, these guides do not go below the level of minor civil divisions. As Healy has pointed out, it is necessary to use the Census Bureau's GBF/DIME file for coding administrative returns to tract levels, currently a difficult and expensive task. Moreover, at present, GBF/DIME files do not exist for all metropolitan areas; after 1980, they will be available for only about 65 percent of the U.S. population.

COVERAGE PROBLEMS

Coverage problems, those associated with the lack of representativeness of IRS returns of actual populations, are varied and have not been adequately studied. There is, in the first place, the question of whether a high or consistent proportion of the population files income tax returns. Almost 90 million persons or families file income tax returns each year, a number that is approaching half the population. Still there are geographic areas in which nearly everyone is covered as a filer or a dependent, and there are others where relatively few people file returns. The problem, of course, is not only the completeness of filing, but the constancy of the ratio between exemptions on IRS returns and total population. We know very little about the volatility of this index, especially in areas of high in- or high out-migration, exactly the areas for which estimation is most difficult. Nor do we know the effect that inflation has in moving the lowest income people to a level at which they must file a return.

The coverage problem may seem at first glance to be staggering, but there are ways out. For example, by estimating for larger areas and adjusting the estimates for component parts to that total, an increase in accuracy of estimates may be achieved. Another is the improvement of locational guides; better still would be a request on IRS forms for more detailed addresses in terms of township as well as county. Whereas people do not necessarily know the township or other minor civil division in which they live, they do have to determine these things when they vote, and such information could be provided for tax-payers as well as for voters by local authorities.

USE OF NON-IRS ADMINISTRATIVE RECORDS

IRS records are not the only ones that can be used to improve the estimates for small areas. States maintain records that can be used, though these have not always been committed to tape. Localities also maintain records that would be valuable. Of special value are the files of housing units, which can be updated through utility or other records, and occasionally checked by ground reconnaissance. Rives has developed such a method, and the housing unit method has been extensively used in Wisconsin—a pioneer among the states in the use of state and local records for population estimation.

It may not be necessary to utilize non-IRS records in all localities. There are areas for which the IRS estimates of migration are good. These areas have been described as suburban, middle-class, tax-filing, and served by a single post office. For other areas, it would seem that the use of an alternative set of administrative records, perhaps one keyed to a political area rather than to zip code would serve as a useful alternative.

NEED FOR LOCAL COOPERATION

It was pointed out that population estimation is in some ways like weather forecasting. While a standard method, employed by a central agency, can make useful forecasts and may adequately characterize most small areas, there are local peculiarities that are difficult to take into account from afar. For that reason local cooperation is essential. People on the spot should know what is happening in the immediate vicinity, and they have local records that permit them to check the routinely made estimates. Healy pointed out that when estimates are presented to local authorities for checking, they often make corrections that are valid. Such cooperation is especially useful for the smallest areas, and it is exactly these for which the percentage error tends to be greatest. Furthermore, as local authorities become more aware of the nature and importance of population estimates they will seek to improve their own abilities to keep track of the population. While there is always the possibility that local authorities will be most anxious to correct figures when they represent a monetary or political loss, we can depend upon them to bring pressures upon the Census Bureau and upon the Congress to improve population estimations, perhaps even to fund a quinquennial census in order to remove some of the uncertainties that will be apparent. Thus, one of the results of revenue sharing and the attention paid to population by federal agencies and the courts will surely be a continuing search for ways of improving postcensal estimates, particularly for small areas. The movement toward handing over to the states some of the federal responsibilities for local areas will have little effect upon the need for small area data. Indeed, the states may increase their efforts in population estimation in order to meet their new responsibilities, a burden the courts will keep them from shirking.

Part Three

Using Synthetic Procedures

5

Private Sector Methods

Peter K. Francese

Estimating demographic variables for small areas has been taking place in the United States since shortly after the 1970 Census. There have been some who said that this activity would become obsolete with the advent of a mid-decade census. With a census every five years there would no longer be a need for sophisticated small area estimates; straight line approximations would suffice for the few years between quinquennial censuses.

However, it is now evident that the 1985 mid-decade census has been cancelled. The reason for not having this census is primarily its enormous cost (estimates have been in the vicinity of $500 million), but also the widespread availability of computerized administration records that can be used for population estimates. Whatever the reason, the result is that far from being obsolete, techniques of estimation will be in even greater demand in the next decade as more public and private sector organizations rely on up-to-date information.

Editors' Note: This chapter by Peter K. Francese is a summary and explication of the conference paper, which dealt with synthetic models used by the private sector in estimating population characteristics. Mr. Francese graciously substituted at the last moment for Mr. Vladimir Almendinger, who was unable to attend. Accordingly, the discussion of the private sector synthetic estimation procedures that follows Mr. Francese's paper reflects the information presented at the conference and not the revised paper.

Demographic estimation takes place on at least two levels. First, there are local estimates generally made by a unit of government for its own area. These estimates, along with short-term projections, are most often used for planning and are occasionally used to attract business. Such estimates are relatively easy to produce since the producers are likely to have intimate knowledge of their area and access to such local records as building permits, utility records, property tax records, school enrollment figures, and any local survey data. However, since the person making the estimates may rely more on his "knowledge" of the area than the hard data, such estimates are subject to considerable bias. Also, lack of objectivity on the part of local government officials sometimes causes the figures to be "adjusted" to reflect what is desired rather than what is factual. Finally, there are few estimation techniques that can be easily understood and readily applied by local officials. However, the papers presented at the Small Area Estimation Conference sponsored by the National Institute of Mental Health, as well as recent work by the Bureau of the Census, provide local officials better tools to work with.

The second level of small area estimation is the national one. There are a number of organizations that create, from one location, small area estimates of demographic data for many localities—in some cases, all U.S. communities. One such organization is, of course, the Bureau of the Census. They must make annual estimates of population and per capita income for each of 39,000 local governmental units that receive revenue-sharing money. Their job is made somewhat easier by their access to confidential Internal Revenue Service and Social Security Administration records and the availability of several million dollars to process them. Another type of organization that makes local estimates is the private company that prepares small area demographic estimates and projections primarily for marketing purposes.

All national estimates of small area data differ from the local estimates in four important ways. First, the indicators available at the local level (e.g., building permits) are not useful for national estimates of small areas because they cannot be obtained uniformly nationwide. Second, the individuals making the national estimates have little if any personal knowledge of the local areas and are not likely to "adjust" the figures accordingly. Third, because there are so many local areas to prepare estimates for, it is unlikely that the national estimator has any vested interest in the final figures. Therefore, any bias that occurs is probably statistical in nature. Fourth, national estimates made by private firms are most often used for evaluating a local area for its market potential, suitability for a retail site, or for calculating market penetration.

Because tens of billions of federal dollars are distributed partly on the basis of Census Bureau population and income estimates, a high degree of accuracy is necessary. In contrast, the marketing potential of a locality depends on many uncertain variables other than demographic ones (e.g., amount and effectiveness of advertising, size of store), a high level of accuracy of the demographic estimates is neither expected nor provided.

But small area demographic estimates are only one of many inputs to a private investment decision involving at most a few million dollars. Consequently, small area estimates for marketing purposes can seldom be sold for more than a few thousand dollars. The end result is that the total production cost of these estimates cannot exceed $50,000 to $100,000. This is a small sum, considering the complexity of estimating demographic data for the many communities in the United States.

The geographic unit for which such estimates are most commonly made is the census tract inside Standard Metropolitan Statistical Areas (SMSAs) and minor civil divisions elsewhere. There are currently about 35,000 census tracts in SMSAs and 25,000 minor civil divisions (MCDs) or census county divisions (CCDs)[1] outside SMSAs. These small geographic areas have the advantage of nesting to county totals. Further, census tracts are all about the same size (4000 persons or so) and are designed to be socially and economically homogeneous. Finally, all tracts and minor civil divisions can be located easily on published Census Bureau maps.

This chapter will describe a method in commercial use today for estimating demographic variables for the small areas described above. The method described is not exclusive; there may be others in use. But this method has produced estimates adequate for the purposes for which they were intended.

The demographic variables to be discussed here are those most heavily in demand—total population, total number of households, and household income. The method to be described works for other variables as well.

ESTIMATING TOTAL POPULATION OF SMALL AREAS

Population estimates for large areas are either simple extrapolations of past trends or are variations on the basic formula of births minus deaths plus or minus migration. These methods work well for large governmental units such as states where vital statistics are available and other administrative records can be used. For small areas such as census tracts or minor civil divisions, however, another method must be developed because no vital statistics or other such data are available. Such small area estimates are often called "synthetic" because they are not made on the basis of any direct evidence; instead they rely on inference from regression formulas.

Let's look at a typical census tract. It has about 4000 persons and is about two square miles in area. The only direct measure of the population is a census every ten years. The boundaries are usually not fixed from decade to decade; census tracts are often split into two or more pieces. However, census tracts do not cross county boundaries; and as noted they always nest to SMSA boundaries. Except in New England, they nest to county boundaries. Therefore they are nested components of larger areas for which we have annual population estimates through the Census Bureau's federal/state cooperative program and the revenue-sharing program.

An estimates program for census tracts (and MCDs where there are no tracts) rests on the basic assumption that the growth pattern for areas with similar demographic character- istics will be similar.

Based on this assumption the next step is to develop regres- sion formulas to predict from tracts with known growth rates the growth of similar tracts where the rates are unknown. This is why these methods are called synthetic—there is no direct evidence of actual growth or decline, only an expectation of such based on the characteristics of the tract. The first national estimates of population and households for census tracts and minor civil divisions were prepared under the author's super- vision late in 1973 at the National Planning Data Corporation. The method used at that time was relatively simple and with some modifications was used by that company until the 1980 Census approached. The following description of how to pre- pare small area population and housing estimates generally follows the way it was done by the above firm during the early seventies.

BASIC TECHNIQUE

In a noncensus year, some municipalities request (and pay for) special censuses, and many local governments make small area population estimates from utility records, building permits, and related data. Also, the Census Bureau makes population estimates for local governments that receive revenue-sharing monies. The basic technique is to prepare a file of demographic data that seem to be predictors of population change. Then by using census tracts for which there is a known population change, see if these variables predict that change. An important part of this technique is the development of predictor variables. A review of the literature in the early seventies revealed that very few attempts had been made to estimate population for small areas, but there were a number of articles on how neigh- borhoods change. When a neighborhood is in the early stages of growth, the dwelling units are new, population relatively young, and density low. As it evolves, both the dwelling units and the population age, the number of persons per household increases and then declines, and the population density reaches its peak. This hypothesis about neighborhood growth and decline led to the choice of variables to be used in the regression analysis.

DATA REQUIREMENTS

To simplify this discussion, the period 1976 to 1980 will be used to illustrate data requirements. The first step is to establish a base file of data for all geographic areas desired. In this case we are referring to census tracts in metropolitan areas and MCDs elsewhere.

A base file for estimating population and households would contain, at minimum, the following items for each tract or MCD:

(1) 1960 population
(2) 1970 population
(3) 1970 households
(4) land area (for computing density)
(5) 1970 Census characteristics
   (a) age data (median, percentage over 65, and so on)
   (b) income data (median and percentage distribution)
   (c) housing value and rent
   (d) age of dwelling units
   (e) type of dwelling units (single- vs. multiple-family)
   (f) vacancy rate
   (g) tenure (owner vs. renter)
   (h) race (percentage black)
   (i) household type (family vs. singles)
   (j) group quarters population
(6) Revenue-sharing data or other updated data

(Some of the census data required will come from the sample questionnaire, so this file cannot be constructed until at least several years after a census.)

The net result will be a 1970 county, SMSA, and state file of population and household data which can be used as control totals for the small area estimates.

The next task is to sum the 1970 population and households for all small areas (tracts or MCDs) up to counties, SMSAs, or states and to check those sums against census final population and household counts to be sure no areas were missed or counted twice. New England presents the biggest problem because tracted areas do not nest to county totals. Though this may seem like a simple matter it presented numerous difficulties that were overcome by using printed reports.[2]

Correction sheets report only revised or "corrected" total population and housing units counts. A revised household count (occupied units only) had to be calculated by prorating the original populations per household over the corrected population counts and checking to make sure the new household figure was slightly less than the corrected housing unit count. In this analysis, crews of vessels were excluded from consideration, since it can be assumed that any population aboard a ship in a harbor counted in a census would no longer be there several years after the census. Therefore, these populations were identified and removed. The 1960 population was compiled by a rather time-consuming map-to-map comparison between 1960 and 1970, and allocating the 1960 population to the 1970 geography of census tract or MCDs. This same work will undoubtedly be done by a private data company which will reconstruct 1970 data for 1980 geography. The land area can be compiled using an electronic planimeter as was done for 1970. The Bureau of the Census is expected to provide this data for the 1980 Census if its budget permits. If the Census Bureau chooses not to create land area for census tracts, a number of private data companies are prepared to do it. The electronic equipment for this task is substantially more advanced today than it was ten years ago so the job of obtaining land area will be easier and cheaper. Once a land area file is prepared it must be merged with the population file. An interesting discovery was that there are a number of census tracts (about 100) that had zero population. Those tracts did not appear on census tapes, and records had to be created for them.

Finally, there is the matter of the date for which estimates are to be prepared. The census, of course, is taken as of the first of April every ten years. County and SMSA population estimates prepared by the Bureau of the Census are as of the thirtieth of June of every year. The population and household estimates can be produced for any date but the first of April is the author's choice, since it corresponds with the date of the census.

An essential part of any small area estimation program is to prepare estimates for the larger areas into which the small areas will fit. In this case estimates must be created for counties, SMSAs, and states. These large area estimates are then used as controls--small area estimates must add up to the larger areas.

There are many sources of county level population estimates. Nearly all of them are published annually. The Census Bureau publishes the federal/state cooperative program estimates for counties, and several private companies independently publish annual estimates of county populations.

It is relatively inexpensive to build up a time series of population estimates for each of the 3138 counties in the United States. For example, in late 1978, Census Bureau estimates would have been published for the years 1971 through 1976 and independent estimates would have been published for every year up to 1978. The procedure is to fit the annual census estimates to a curve, project the figures out to 1978, and compare them with the independent estimates.

In over 90% of the cases, the two estimates will be so close that it does not matter which one is chosen. In those cases where there is a wide disparity, visual examination of the past trend and phone calls to the Census Bureau can resolve the differences.

County estimates can, of course, be summed to SMSAs (except in New England) and states, and put aside for future reconciliation with tract data. Households present a slightly different problem. The Census Bureau produces only state level household estimates, but independent private companies produce annual county level household estimates that match reasonably well with the Census Bureau state estimates. Since there may be differences at the county level between the Census Bureau and independent population estimates, population per household can be calculated using the independent county household estimates and that ratio applied to the county population estimates described above.

In residential areas, two types of populations are found: those that live in households and those that live in group quarters. Because the patterns of change are different for these populations, the population estimates must be made separately. In this chapter we are primarily concerned with the household population.

Since the population in group quarters changes in unpredictable ways (i.e., a school closes, a new hospital is built), it must be estimated separately from the household population. Early in the decade the group quarters population can be assumed to be approximately equal to the census values. Later an estimate of the size of each large group quarters population must be obtained from the agency responsible. For example, Army base personnel counts can be obtained from the Department of Defense, and college and university on-campus populations from the Department of Education.

As noted, the basic method is regression analysis. Consequently, it is important to have a good sample of census tracts for which the present population is known. Ideally, one would choose a stratified random sample of tracts, take a special census in each of them, and then extrapolate to the rest of the tracts on the basis of the results of regression analysis.

In the real world, the expense of a special census prohibits such an approach. Instead, the sample of tracts includes any area where a municipality has conducted a special census for some other purpose or where a municipality has made its own estimates in a careful manner. Occasionally a revenue-sharing area is a single census tract (a small suburban town or village) and can be used in the sample. The problem with this expedient is that the chosen tracts are anything but random. Invariably, it is only growing suburban communities that request special censuses—declining inner cities gladly wait until the next census for the bad news.

Census tract data from special census areas may be obtained from the Special Census Branch of the Census Bureau. However, each local government that does its own estimates must be contacted individually. There are over 300 such agencies and it takes several months to get a response from all of them. After locally done estimates are received they must be evaluated to see if they add up to the previously established county totals. Frequently, they exceed any reasonable number by a wide margin and must be rejected. One very large city prepared estimates showing no census tracts losing population, clearly an exercise in wishful thinking. But in many cases the local agency provides a description of the estimation technique. If their methods use building and demolition permits, vacancy checks, take into account changing household size, and sum to a known county total, then the estimates can be used to establish a regression formula.

The sample of census tracts is randomly separated into two parts; one segment containing one-third of the sample, and the other containing the remainder. The two-thirds part of the sample is then divided into several subsets such as regions of the county, urban and rural areas, SMSA and non-SMSA areas, central city, and remainder of SMSAs.

The data for 1970 and 1960 in the data base for areas corresponding to the two-thirds sample were regressed on the sample data using standard regression computer programs (e.g., BMD, SPSS). The relative predictive ability of each variable in the data base was then tested and promising equations tried on the remaining one-third sample to see how well they predicted population change. With the limited stratifications possible early in the decade, only fifteen to twenty equations were possible. Later in the decade, when many more test tracts were available, thirty to fifty equations were used. In any case, preparing population estimates is an iterative process. Estimates must be checked for reasonableness, checked against county totals, adjusted where necessary, and then rechecked.

After choosing the best regression equations in terms of F-Ratios and R-Squares, the process of testing the limits of each variable can begin. One problem with equations such as these is they can be very sensitive to minute changes in a variable. Let's assume that a percentage of the population over 65 years old is one of the variables in a final equation. All of the test tracts had values between 5 percent and 20 percent, not a particularly large spread. What would happen to an estimate where the proportion of people over 65 was 50 percent or 80 percent, not an unheard of event in Florida? Each variable must be tested for its sensitivity beyond limits of the sample areas, and estimates for tracts with values beyond these limits are either flagged for visual examination or dropped.

After the limits testing, the universe of census tracts is stratified in the same manner as the sample, and the equations are applied to the base data file discussed earlier. Once the initial estimates are prepared, they are summed to counties and compared to the previously determined county totals. If the sum of the tracts deviates from known county totals by more than predetermined tolerance level, say 3 percent, then an examination of the tracts is in order to see if any have grown or declined by some unlikely amount. Thus, the estimate that a tract had declined from 5000 to 500 persons in three years would be examined. In such cases, either another equation can be used or the county growth rate assumed.

Another test is to sort all tracts in the nation by estimated growth, both absolutely and in percentage terms. A visual examination of the top and bottom 1000 and also the distribution of tracts by growth will reveal any major weakness in the method. If for example, three-quarters of the census tracts declined in population when only one-quarter of the test tracts declined, something is clearly wrong with one or more of the equations. Sometimes an examination of the bottom 1000 tracts will reveal several hundred tracts whose populations fell to zero, clearly an unlikely event. Here it may be a matter of one or two variables not being within tolerance levels, or a census tract whose population was so small in 1970 that key variables were suppressed.

Once the final population estimates are prepared, the household estimates can be quickly generated. Since we know population per household figures for each county for both the census year and the estimate year, it is possible to find the percentage change in this statistic for the county. This percentage change is applied to each tract, after which the new tract population per household statistic is divided into the previously calculated tract population to get the household estimates. Finally, it should be remembered that regression estimates work reasonably well only with census tracts, not with MCDs. This may be because census tracts are designed by the Census Bureau to be socioeconomically homogeneous and about the same in population size. MCDs, which vary in population size from a few hundred people to tens of thousands, usually are governmental units and are decidedly not homogeneous. Hence, in the early years after a census, a simple projection of a past trend can be used. Later, the revenue-sharing estimates can be converted into MCDs. This is quite easy in the Northeast but more difficult in the West, where MCDs are not necessarily political entities. Nevertheless, the cost of developing a population and household estimate for each tract and MCD in the country should not exceed $50,000.

It should be recognized that the time between the baseline census and the estimation date affects both the quality of the estimate and the complexity of the estimating procedure. Thus, when the census is recent (as in 1973 or 1974) there are few census tracts for which the present population is known. This is counterbalanced by the fact that in the short time since the census, changes are not very great. However, when the census data are eight or nine years old, updated populations are available for thousands of tracts, but estimates are more difficult because large changes could have occurred over the eight years. Thus the basic techniques for estimating small area population changes become more complicated as the estimation period becomes larger. Initially the procedure simply projects past trends, but when the census data get older it is necessary to develop more sophisticated techniques and rely more on current sources of data. An example of the latter is the use of revenue-sharing estimates. The conversion of estimates from revenue-sharing areas to MCDs and tracts is time consuming and expensive. When such estimates were first published in 1973 they were not considered useful enough to warrant expensive conversion, but by 1978 they became essential ingredients in small area population estimates.

INCOME ESTIMATES

In this section methods used in the private sector to produce low-cost small area income estimates will be presented. There are three measures of money income frequently used in demographic work, all available from the census. They are: per capita income, average household income, and the distribution of household income. A simple method to estimate each is presented below.

PER CAPITA INCOME

This is simply the aggregate income of all persons in a geographic area divided by the total population. The divisor is all persons whether they had income or not. The one great advantage of the per capita figure is that it is one of the variables needed by the revenue-sharing formula and hence is estimated annually by the Census Bureau for each of the approximately 39,000 revenue-sharing entities in the United States. The Census Bureau estimates income by using the Internal Revenue Service and Social Security records coded to the municipal level.

These data are checked against census information. In 1980 the income questions were asked of a very large sample (one out of two households) in communities of less than 2500 to assure statistical validity of the data for small places. In larger places the sample size was one in six.

Estimating per capita income for MCDs outside SMSAs is simply a matter of allocating revenue-sharing areas to the MCDs. Inside SMSAs the estimation of per capita income for census tracts is more complex. The first step is to calculate an aggregate income for a large area (a city or a county). This is done by multiplying the per capita income by the population estimate previously obtained. The next step consists of allocating this aggregate number down to the census tracts using occupational distributions. Specifically, the procedure is to choose some test revenue-sharing areas using the same criteria as in the population estimates program (e.g., region, urban, rural, central city, noncentral city, black, white) and identify the best predictors of income change. It turns out that occupation is a very powerful predictor of income change. Using a set of relatively simple equations based on occupation it is possible to allocate the aggregate income of the larger revenue-sharing area down to the census tract. The last step is to divide the aggregate by the previously calculated population to get the per capita income distribution. The same sorts of checks for reasonableness and variable sensitivity that were done for the population must, of course, be done for per capita income.

AVERAGE HOUSEHOLD INCOME

The average household income is the aggregate income earned by persons in households divided by the number of households. Total income estimates for small areas are obtained as described for per capita income estimates. In the absence of any group quarters population this calculation is simply a matter of dividing aggregate income by the number of households. However, where there are group quarters populations, some of the aggregate income must be allocated to these populations. One way is to allocate to them the same proportion of income as the group had in the decennial census. This will be possible after the 1980 Census, but in the 1970 Census "household" income was not reported. So an average per capita figure for all group quarters population (approximately $1000 a year) had to be used. That figure was multiplied by the group quarters population and the resulting aggregate income was then subtracted from the total aggregate income. Finally, a division by the number of households yields average household income.

INCOME DISTRIBUTION

A procedure often used by the private sector, constant proportion share method, is introduced to illustrate how one might estimate income distributions. The procedure requires that the distribution be known for some large area for both the present and for the past by the census tracts or MCDs that make up the larger area.

The problem in dealing with income is that the income distribution must first be adjusted for inflation. The inflation factors are well known by the Census Bureau and are used to calculate "constant dollar" changes in income. The following example uses the 1976 Survey of Income and Education (SIE) and assumes that, prior to using the estimation procedure, the 1970 income distributions were upgraded to 1976 using an inflation factor of 146.6 percent.

The 1976 SIE was a sample of about 150,000 U.S. households. For reasons of confidentiality, data are available only for geographic areas containing over 250,000 persons. This means that data tabulations can be obtained for only the top 125 SMSAs, the 50 states and several other large areas. The total number of nesting geographic areas available is 197. These 197 units of geography completely cover the United States without overlap.

Since we have 1976 SIE distributions of demographic variables as well as certain 1970 census distributions for each of these 197 areas, the change from 1970 to 1976 can be obtained directly. For example, for the Erie, Pennsylvania SMSA it is possible to obtain a distribution of household income in 1970 from the census and a distribution of household income in 1976 from the SIE. Therefore, the changes in each element of that distribution can be calculated.

The task is to take the change in each element of the distribution and allocate it to each census tract in the Erie SMSA. In order to allocate to tracts the changes in household income, certain assumptions must be made. These are necessary because we lack data beyond 1970 for small geographic areas. Most of these assumptions (such as uniform inflation rates) apply to individual data items. The most important assumption is that any demographic distribution by tract (excluding total population and total households) was the same for the SMSA in 1976 as it was in 1970. Stated differently, the total change from 1970 to 1976 in any variable at the large geographic levels is allocated to smaller geographic levels by assuming that the ratio between the smaller and larger units has remained constant since 1970. Total population and total households are not considered as variables for the purposes of the above assumption. We have already estimated how they have changed at the tract level since 1970. (For details about SIE file structure for this example, see Appendix 5.1).

Since we assume that each census tract is a constant proportion of its SMSA, the application of this assumption is known as the "constant proportion share method." This method involves the calculation of updating factors at the SMSA level and applying them uniformly to all tracts in the SMSA. This method is straightforward for SMSAs with SIE data. For SMSAs smaller than 250,000 and for non-SMSA areas, the procedure is more complex.

The complexity is best illustrated by the example of Pennsylvania. In the SIE, 10 SMSAs covering 25 counties in Pennsylvania are identified; 2 small tracted SMSAs (two counties) are identified as the "metropolitan state remainder." Finally, 1 partially tracted county and 39 untracted counties are identified (in total) as "nonmetropolitan state remainder." Each county must be identified by the SIE areas in which it is included; tracts and/or MCDs in each of those counties must be treated appropriately.

The constant proportion share method can be used to update other distributions such as home value, rent, and persons per unit.

NOTES

1. For simplicity of presentation, MCDs and CCDs in states not having MCDs will be referred to as MCDs.
2. The Bureau of Census did not prepare a master file with "final and official" population counts for the 1970 Census. Such a file had to be created by referring to correction sheets, the printed reports (PC[1] Characteristics of the Population and PHC[1] Census Tracts), and occasionally, Census Bureau memoranda.

APPENDIX 5.1

Four files are necessary to update tract and MCD level demographic data. These are:

(1) Tract/MCD file of 1970 data
(2) 197 SIE area file of 1970 data
(3) 197 SIE area file of 1976 data
(4) Current population and household counts for tracts and MCDs and the 197 SIE areas

The basic steps to be performed on each of these files are:

(1) Merge File A with the most recent estimates of population and households available (File D). Eliminate all tracts or MCDs for which no estimates are available, and create zero filled records for all cases where there are estimates of population and households but no 1970 census data.
(2) Sum all of the data (from step one above) to create the 1970 SIE area totals (File B).

(3) Merge the 1970 SIE area file with the 1976 SIE data for the same areas (Files B and C) and calculate 1970-1976 SMSA level updating factors.

(4) Merge the SIE area file created in 3 above with the tract file so that an SIE area total precedes the tract/MCD records for that area.

(5) Calculate updated variables for each tract/MCD according to the following instructions:

(a) Prepare for each tract/MCD the distributions for which SIE level updating factors were calculated.

(b) Multiply each element in those distributions by the appropriate SIE level updating factors (f) and sum the revised distribution to obtain a total.

(c) Divide this sum (Ar) into the independently obtained estimate of populations, households or other variable (Au) and multiply the result (F) by each element in the revised distribution.

Tract Distribution		SIE Update Factors		Revised Distribution		Final Adjustment		Updated Distribution
A_1	x	f_1	=	Ar_1	x	F	=	Au_1
A_2	x	f_2	=	Ar_2	x	F	=	Au_2
A_3	x	f_3	=	Ar_3	x	F	=	Au_3
A_4	x	f_4	=	Ar_4	x	F	=	Au_4
A_5	x	f_5	=	Ar_5	x	F	=	Au_5

$$F = A_u/A_r$$

6

Evaluation and Synopsis

The Editors

THE PURPOSE OF THE
PRIVATE SECTOR SYNTHETIC MODELS

When evaluating the private synthetic models such as those presented by Peter K. Francese, one must keep in mind that the goals of these models are clearly different from the administrative record procedures previously discussed. Whereas the Bureau was concerned with developing highly accurate estimates that could be used to allocate funds, the private sector synthetic models are concerned with providing a reasonably accurate estimate for a market or service area composed of small census areas (census tracts or MCDs). Considerable error in estimates for small areas can be tolerated in these models, if, on the average, the small area estimates are reasonable. Then, the estimates for the market or service areas will also be reasonable.

GIVEN GOALS, WHAT PROBLEMS

Two kinds of basic types of problems emerge with the private sector synthetic models—those related to the assumption that similar areas change in similar ways and those related to the sample areas used to develop regression models. These are discussed below.

SIMILAR AREAS HAVE SIMILAR PATTERNS OF CHANGE

The basic assumption of the synthetic models is that areas, specifically census tracts, with similar demographic characteristics can be expected to change in a similar manner. To achieve an appropriate level of area similarity, it was necessary to control the small geographic areas by economic status, percentage rural, region density, occupational status, and perhaps some additional social area dimensions. How far one needs to go requires further exploration. To the extent possible, the social area characteristics of racial and ethnic populations should be considered separately. Of the socioeconomic dimensions, occupation status, because of its stability across time, should be an essential part of any model.

The need to control density was clearly recognized by Francese and other conference participants. They noted that important problems were associated with density. The problems were associated with the type of small area being considered. In suburban single-dwelling detached areas, density—particularly net density—increased the adequacy of the regression models. Such areas have an upper limit of potential growth. In part, this reflects zoning patterns that precluded the building of large apartment complexes. In areas with large numbers of apartment houses, it is difficult to determine an upper limit of potential growth since the building of new structures may radically change the population and density of an area.

While there may be some tendency for demographically similar areas to experience similar types of change, this is, of course, not always the case. It was pointed out that different residential locations (i.e., suburb vs. central city) can easily influence the direction of change of comparatively homogeneous areas. For example, residential areas with predominately white child-rearing populations in the suburbs tend to change in easily predictable ways—generally the immigration of similar populations and the aging of existing populations. Net density provides information about population change in such areas. However, in the central cities that are becoming predominately black, such conditions are not often observed. For example, to the extent that student populations in city school systems become predominately lower-class and black, and the schools are integrated through busing programs, significant numbers of middle-rank childrearing white couples may leave their city single-dwelling detached housing units for similar suburban sites. They will be replaced by populations with significantly different characteristics. Such mobility could not be estimated from knowledge of the demographic characteristics of small homogeneous geographic areas alone, particularly if sample areas upon which estimation equations were derived were from suburban areas.

Moreover, not only does one have to consider the location of an area within an SMSA, but also the demographic characteristics of the small areas that surround a small area. David Birch points out that the character of such areas may be a significant clue to the direction of change within a given small area (see Chapter 11, this volume).

It was also emphasized during the discussion that racial and ethnic demographic characteristics need to be controlled. To the extent that the lifestyles of blacks, or other racial and ethnic populations, and whites in similar social and economic class positions are significantly different, estimating the expected change in black or other racial or ethnic populations on the basis of the characteristics of white populations will result in estimates that have high error levels.

SAMPLE PROBLEMS

The fact that the private sector synthetic models are forced to rely on a nonrandom set of areas creates serious problems for the validity and reliability of estimates. The sample areas available for two periods of time tend to be suburban or small city tracts and predominately white. The changes experienced in such areas cannot be expected to provide adequate estimates for central city areas, minority populations or other areas outside the bounds of the area used in the sample. However, it is worth noting that to the extent that the private sector synthetic estimates are used to locate and identify the characteristics of white suburban and small city populations (i.e., affluent populations), the estimates may be adequate. For areas not containing these populations, such an estimation may be inadequate.

One way of improving private sector synthetic models would be to introduce the use of sequential sampling procedures, a procedure not often used in the social sciences. Once a regression model has been established for areas on the basis of the available nonrandom sample of census tracts or MCDs, a sequential sampling procedure might be introduced to determine the generality of the model. It should be noted that while not as rigorous as sequential sampling, private synthetic models are iteratively tested for adequacy. For example, results are checked against other data or the best available key informants from a local area.

In conclusion, the private sector synthetic models are simple, perhaps naive, and are low cost. In the short run they provide good estimates, particularly for areas outside the central cities. Where appropriate to the need, it is probably not necessary to employ more sophisticated models. In fact, naive models may often provide estimates as good as more sophisticated and expensive models. When this appears to be the case, the naive models are, of course, the most appropriate models to employ.

Part Four

Using Survey Methods

7

Assessment of a Survey Approach

Norfleet W. Rives, Jr.

The growing presence of population estimates in planning and public policy underscores the importance of using statistically defensible procedures to prepare these estimates. Demographers recognize two basic approaches to population estimation. The first approach involves methods that are essentially mathematical in nature and that treat population as a time-dependent numerical aggregate. The methods of this approach are generally well known (Spiegelman, 1968). The second approach incorporates a series of methods collectively based on the concept of component estimation. The methods of this approach are concerned with the estimation of current population through either (1) direct estimation of the actual components of population growth—fertility, mortality, and migration, or (2) identification of symptomatic indicators or covariates of demographic change (Morrison, 1971). Mathematical methods for population estimation are more conveniently and economically applied in particular situations because their data requirements and computational demands are quite modest. Component methods are capable of greater accuracy, at least in principle, because they explicitly recognize the processes governing population growth.

The population estimation procedure presented in this chapter follows demographic tradition to the extent that it involves the use of one of the most elementary models of demographic

change. The procedure differs from more conventional demographic methods, however, to the extent that it incorporates
direct measures of population growth obtained through survey
research. Most population estimates are produced without the
benefit of direct observation. The accuracy of these estimates
cannot be satisfactorily established without the use of census
counts or similar benchmark information. The procedure presented in this chapter permits a closer monitoring of the growth
process. The cost of this approach will exceed the cost of more
conventional demographic procedures, but the benefits associated with direct measures of population change may very well
justify the greater expenditure.

METHODOLOGY

The survey approach to population estimation permits the
estimation of both total population and population characteristics. The method is intended for use in smaller geographic
units, generally administrative and statistical units below the
state level, such as counties, incorporated places, minor civil
divisions, school districts, and health service areas.

The geographic unit considered in this chapter is the minor
civil division (MCD). The MCD is the principal subdivision of a
county. The census county division (CCD) performs the MCD
function in states without MCD designations. County planning
departments frequently use the MCD as a planning analysis area,
the basic area for which numerous physical and social plans are
developed.

ESTIMATING TOTAL POPULATION

The estimation procedure for total population involves a
five-stage process. The first stage requires the user to divide the
MCD into a large number of relatively small geographic units.
These units represent clusters and constitute the MCD cluster
sampling frame. The second stage requires the user to draw a

sample of clusters at random from the cluster population. This sample is designated the "benchmark sample" in the estimation procedure. The benchmark sample should be drawn to coincide with the timing of a census count, since the basic model of the estimation procedure involves population change between a census (benchmark) date and the postcensal current date of the population estimate. The benchmark sample for estimates beyond 1980, for example, would be drawn to coincide with the timing of the 1980 Census. A benchmark sample could also be drawn to coincide with the timing of a special census. Considerations surrounding the design of the MCD cluster sampling frame and the selection of sample clusters are reserved for a subsequent discussion.

The third stage of the estimation procedure requires the user to enumerate the household population of the benchmark sample. Each household must provide information on the number of persons who usually reside at that address, following the census definition of usual residence. If the estimation procedure is also to be used for population characteristics, the respondent should be asked to provide the necessary information for each household member. The reference date for questions on household size and other characteristics should be the census date. If the benchmark sample were drawn to coincide with the timing of the 1980 Census, for example, then respondents would be asked to provide information for April 1, 1980.

The use of a postcensal survey with a census reference date may produce some distortion in the sample information, to the extent that household migration and mortality operate to change the demographic structure of the MCD between the reference date and the time of the survey. If the survey is conducted soon after the census date, however, the consequences of this effect for the representativeness of sample information are probably negligible.

The fourth stage of the estimation procedure requires the user to replicate the entire sampling operation associated with the benchmark sample at the time the population estimate is to be prepared. This second sample is designated the "*update* sample." Suppose a population estimate is to be computed for July 1, 1982. This date is the reference date for the update sample. The benchmark sample will have been drawn to coincide with the timing of either the 1980 Census or a more recent special census. The household population in the *same* clusters used for the benchmark sample is enumerated a second time, with respondents providing all information for the 1982 reference date. Some households will be larger the second time, while others will be smaller. Some will be new to the area, while others will have disappeared. The net effect is sample evidence of population change.

The final stage of the estimation procedure is the computation stage. Let x_i be the enumerated household population of the ith cluster in the benchmark sample, and let y_i be the enumerated population of the *same* cluster in the update sample. The total household population associated with the former sample is X, the sum of the x_i values over all sample clusters, and the total population associated with the latter sample is Y, the sum of the y_i values over all sample clusters. If P_c is the MCD household population in the most recent census, then the postcensal current estimate P_e of the MCD household population for the reference date of the update sample is given by the expression:

$$P_e = (Y/X)P_c \qquad [1]$$

The quotient (Y/X) is a ratio estimator of the growth of the household population during the postcensal period.

The population estimate P_e is subject to the sampling and nonsampling errors of the ratio estimator and the coverage errors of the census count P_c. Sampling errors can be regulated quite effectively through the use of an efficient sample design, while nonsampling errors can be regulated to some extent through the vigorous enforcement of quality control procedures. Census coverage errors constitute an entirely different problem. National estimates of census coverage have been prepared by the Bureau of the Census, but the Bureau has not been able to produce estimates of comparable quality for states and local areas, despite a rather substantial research investment (U.S. Bureau of the Census, 1977). This suggests that census errors below the national level will just have to be tolerated; there is simply no sufficient basis for their adjustment.

When the number of sample clusters can be considered large, generally beyond thirty, and this produces coefficients of variation for household population per cluster that are relatively small, generally less than 10 percent, then the ratio estimator (Y/X) is approximately normally distributed in repeated sampling (Cochran, 1977). Under these conditions, the large-sample population variance for the estimator P_e is given by the expression:

$$N^2(1 - f) \Sigma (y_i - Rx_i)^2/n(N - 1) \qquad [2]$$

where N is the number of clusters in the MCD sampling frame, n is the number of clusters in both the benchmark and update samples, R is the population (true) growth ratio for the postcensal period, and f is the cluster sampling fraction (n/N). Equation 2 implicitly assumes simple random sampling. The sample estimator for the population variance of P_e can be written in the form:

$$N^2(1 - f) \Sigma (y_i - rx_i)^2/n(n - 1) \qquad [3]$$

where r is the sample growth ratio for the postcensal period. Equation 3 is an approximate expression; the bias is of the order $(1/n)$.

The survey approach to population estimation provides an estimate only of the population in households. An estimate of total resident population requires information on the population in group quarters. If the MCD group quarters population is small relative to total resident population, and this is typically the case, then the group quarters count in the most recent census may actually be a useful estimate. If the group quarters population of an MCD is relatively large, however, then it will

almost always have a primary source, such as a college or
university, a correctional facility, or a military installation.
Information on the size of such populations, even below the
county level, can normally be obtained from the appropriate
institutional officials.

ESTIMATING POPULATION CHARACTERISTICS

Total population represents one dimension of demographic
change. Population composition represents another. The survey
approach to population estimation can be applied to numerous
demographic, economic, and social characteristics. The method
can even be extended to produce characteristic detail for households and housing units. Any population or housing variable for
which information can be collected in a household survey can
technically be estimated using the procedure presented in this
chapter.

The following characteristics might be considered important
for small area analysis and monitoring:

(1) age-sex-race composition
(2) low-income population
(3) primary-individual population
(4) female-householder population
(5) single-family detached housing units

The first characteristic constitutes the basic demographic profile. An age-sex distribution can be estimated for *total* population or a particular race category. The age-sex distribution for
total population will be the most stable, given the well-known
limitations of sample estimators. An age-sex distribution for the
black population might have to be aggregated to broad age
groups before the distribution could be considered stable. This
modification will almost always be necessary for areas in which
the black population (or any population subgroup) is relatively
small. Standards promulgated by the Bureau of the Census for

the tabulation of survey information can serve as useful guidelines. These standards are found in census volumes and numerous other reports, especially those based on the Current Population Survey (U.S. Bureau of the Census, 1978).

The estimation procedure for population characteristics, like the procedure for total population, includes the possibility of confidence intervals. Indeed, the ability to summarize errors of estimation in a direct and systematic fashion is a unique feature of the survey approach. Most population estimation techniques, particularly demographic techniques, permit only statements of error that tend to be judgmental in nature. Such statements can be useful, but they do not always have a strong empirical basis. Interval estimates using the survey approach are constructed in the usual manner. Point estimators for both total population and population characteristics are approximately normally distributed under simple random sampling.

One final point concerning the estimation of characteristic detail deserves attention. This point involves the relation of detail in the update sample to the corresponding detail in the most recent census. There is a tendency among users of census statistics to abandon the information with the passage of time. The figures clearly become dated, and questions arise concerning their continued usefulness. These questions are frequently answered in a purely speculative manner; a persistent suspicion of "old figures," however unsubstantiated, leads to their casual, and sometimes premature, dismissal. A more systematic approach to the evaluation of the continuing utility of census statistics might involve the use of the update sample in a hypothesis-testing framework. The purpose of this approach is to determine whether the update sample presents sufficient evidence to indicate that the structure of characteristics in the most recent census is no longer valid. The null hypothesis of the test procedure would specify that no change has occurred during the postcensal period. The alternative hypothesis would specify that the update sample was not drawn from the census universe with respect to the characteristic of interest. If the null hypothesis were rejected, then the estimate from the update sample would be used rather than the summary measure from the census. If the hypothesis were accepted, however, then the figure in the most recent census might still be appropriate for postcensal applications. There is no reason to abandon census statistics just because they are dated. The population and housing counts may no longer be valid, owing to postcensal growth, but this does not necessarily imply that structural relations have changed.

ILLUSTRATION

The survey approach to population estimation can be illustrated with the following example. The sample information used in the example is based on recent growth patterns of minor civil divisions in Anne Arundel County, a metropolitan county of the Baltimore SMSA. Since the actual field surveys necessary to generate the benchmark and update samples could not be conducted for obvious reasons, the sample information has been designed to simulate the mechanics of the estimation procedure.

The example involves the estimation of the total resident population of a hypothetical MCD for a midyear date two years following the most recent census. The household population of the area at the time of the census is 50,000. The MCD has been divided into 1000 mutually exclusive, completely exhaustive geographic clusters (primary sampling units). The average cluster size is 50. A simple random sample of 30 clusters is drawn to coincide with the timing of the census. This sample is the benchmark sample, according to the procedure discussed in the previous section. An enumeration of sample clusters produces 1485 household residents; there are 505 sample households. Table 7.1 shows the simulated cluster distribution of the sample household population.

The sampling operation is replicated for the *same* 30 clusters to coincide with the reference date of the population estimate. The replication generates the update sample. An enumeration of sample clusters produces 1560 residents; there are 557 sample households (see Table 7.1).

TABLE 7.1   Enumerated Household Populations of Sample Clusters for
Hypothetical Benchmark and Update Samples

Cluster Number	Benchmark Population	Update Population	Cluster Number	Benchmark Population	Update Population
1	42	45	16	40	43
2	45	47	17	52	53
3	45	48	18	47	49
4	48	49	19	40	44
5	47	52	20	51	53
6	56	59	21	55	56
7	60	63	22	41	42
8	59	61	23	58	62
9	46	47	24	49	53
10	53	56	25	43	47
11	58	60	26	54	57
12	42	43	27	42	46
13	50	51	28	60	63
14	57	59	29	47	49
15	42	46	30	56	57

The ratio estimate for total growth equals the population in the update sample (1560) divided by the population in the benchmark sample (1485). The estimated ratio is 1.051, representing an average annual growth rate of 2.2 percent. The ratio estimate applied to the MCD census count (50,000) yields the estimated household population. The estimate is 52,550, following equation 1. If the estimated population in group quarters on the postcensal reference date were 1,250, then the estimate for total resident population would be 53,800.

The standard deviation of the household population estimate is approximately 232, following equation 3. The coefficient of variation for average cluster size (population per cluster) is 13.3 percent for the benchmark sample and 12.6 percent for the update sample. Since both values are near 10 percent, and the number of sample clusters (30) can be considered large by statistical standards, the household population estimator is approximately normally distributed. The limits of a 95 percent interval estimate for MCD household population on the post-censal date are 52,086 and 53,014. Since these limits define a relatively small range, one can be reasonably sure that the point estimate is quite useful. Well-designed surveys should yield interval estimates that are tolerably large.

DISCUSSION

Two considerations surrounding the use of the survey approach to population estimation warrant special attention. The first consideration involves the sampling procedure, and the second consideration involves cost.

SAMPLING PROCEDURE

Concern for the sampling procedure presumes a concern for statistical precision. The design of the cluster sampling frame and the selection of sample units influence the accuracy of the estimates for total population and population characteristics.

The cluster sampling frame should consist of a large number of relatively small geographic units. A sampling frame with many clusters will facilitate drawing samples that provide reasonably good coverage of the study area and produce estimators with desirable statistical properties (Cochran, 1977). Furthermore, since the population estimation procedure requires cluster enumeration rather than subsampling, the use of geographic units that are too large might create unnecessary logistical problems.

One method of frame construction for single-stage cluster sampling at the local level involves the use of property assessment maps. The current map series for a metropolitan county can normally be obtained from the county engineering department. Since these maps are used on a regular basis for mandated purposes, they can be expected to contain the most recent information on county geography. The typical map series will delineate the boundaries of both administrative and statistical areas. These include minor civil divisions, census tracts, blocks, incorporated places, school districts, water service areas, transportation zones, and modified map grids.

A popular primary sampling unit at the local level is the block. The block is a useful area for several reasons. First, block boundaries are relatively easy to identify on the ground, and they are generally considered somewhat more permanent than the boundaries of other small units. Second, block populations are not so large that their enumeration can be expected to create difficult logistical problems. Third, the block statistics program of the decennial census has encouraged metropolitan cities and counties throughout the United States to extend formal block designation beyond the urbanized area, providing a more comprehensive system of small geographic units for administrative and statistical purposes.

Constructing cluster sampling frames from local property maps, although a seemingly simple process, can involve a substantial investment of time, energy, and money. Furthermore, despite its apparent usefulness as a primary sampling unit in larger cities and counties, the block may not be the most effective unit in smaller areas, such as census tracts and minor civil divisions. If a primary sampling unit below the block level becomes necessary, its selection from property maps may prove extremely tedious. Alternative approaches to frame construction should be explored, approaches that combine economic considerations with greater convenience and flexibility. The following approach is one possibility.

The block network in many metropolitan areas has been used to construct an automated information system incorporating statistics from both the census and local sources. The system, a product of Census Bureau technology, is called the GBF/DIME System (Silver, 1977). The basic ingredient of the system is the GBF/DIME File, a computerized version of a street map containing all the features shown on the Census Bureau Metropolitan Map Series, plus block-by-block address ranges, zip codes, and geographic coordinate values at intersections. Each record in the file identifies a segment of a feature on the map sheet, the two "nodal points" between which it is located, the corresponding address ranges, and the geographic units on both sides of the street. The address range on each side of the street (the "block face") is technically an elementary unit of a block. This range could serve as a primary sampling unit in areas where entire blocks might be too large. Address ranges could also be aggregated to produce clusters that deviate from the basic block configuration of an area. Since the GBF/DIME System covers all address ranges within a given universe, some ranges will contain commercial or industrial properties. If a particular range exhibits a high concentration of these properties, and there is no reason to expect residential growth in the area, then the range might be excluded from the frame. The GBF/DIME File is sufficiently flexible to permit such modifications.

One criticism of the GBF/DIME System is its failure to cover all segments of some metropolitan areas. Recognizing the importance of a consistent, comprehensive geocoding scheme for each metropolitan city and county, the Census Bureau has initiated the CUE Program, a cooperative effort on the part of Bureau personnel and local officials to correct, update, and extend the coverage of the GBF/DIME System. Agencies in 180 of the 196 metropolitan areas that originally constructed a file are now working on file revisions. Another 70 areas that did not participate in the original program are in the process of building files. Much of the work on new files has already been completed.

Once the cluster sampling frame has been constructed, sample clusters for the benchmark sample can be drawn at random to coincide with the timing of a census count. The sampling procedure follows statistical convention. Each cluster in the sampling frame is assigned a unique identification number from 1 to N, where N is the total number of clusters in the frame, and a randomizing device is then used to select the sample clusters. The update sample does not require a second sampling operation, only a second enumeration of the clusters from the benchmark sample to coincide with the reference date of the population estimate.

COST CONSIDERATIONS

The survey approach to population estimation requires the usual expenditures associated with survey research. The major expenditure categories cover survey design and sample selection, fieldwork, and information processing. The first category, survey design and sample selection, involves the preparation of the survey instrument, the construction of the sampling frame, and the drawing of sample clusters. Since the questions required for the estimation of total population and standard population characteristics appear on the census schedule, the cost of designing the survey instrument should be negligible. Furthermore, since census items have been subjected to extensive testing and evaluation, there is really no need for a survey pretest, unless the user wants to examine survey procedure. But even in this case, the need for a procedural pretest can be eliminated with minimal interviewer training and effective survey organization. The only potentially significant design expenditure is the cost of new questions having no performance record. Such questions will have to be developed and subjected to adequate testing.

The cost of constructing the cluster sampling frame should be quite reasonable in areas where the GBF/DIME System is available. If the file completely covers the study universe, then the primary sampling units can be developed from address ranges (block faces). The GBF/DIME File will have to be passed several times; once to establish file structure, and again to create clusters. Information on file structure may be available from local officials, saving the expense of a computer run. If a GBF/DIME System is not available for the study area, or the existing system covers only certain area segments, then a separate sampling frame will have to be constructed either for the entire area or for the uncovered segments. The cost of this work could be quite high, depending upon the quality of local property maps, the size of the area in question, and the amount of clustering that must be done. Since alternative methods of population estimation are available in every area, the use of the method presented in this chapter might be prudently restricted to areas having either a comprehensive GBF/DIME System or an equivalent geocoding framework.

The cost of sample selection is simply the cost of passing the frame. If the frame is automated, and a random number generator is available, the cost will be minimal. If the frame must be sampled manually, the cost of drawing a given sample may be somewhat greater.

The major cost of the survey approach to population estimation is the cost of fieldwork, and the major cost of fieldwork is the cost of interviewing, a cost the user must incur not only for the benchmark sample, but also for each update sample. Interview expenditures can be minimized to some extent through the use of relatively inexperienced personnel. Since the questions necessary to estimate both total population and standard characteristics are not difficult to administer, especially following an effective interviewer training session, there is really no need to recruit persons with impressive credentials.

The interviewing process for population estimation is very straightforward. Interviewers must visit each household in the sample address ranges they have been assigned, conduct the interview with a competent respondent, or make arrangements to return at a later date if such a person is not at home. The determination of vacant units can be made through rental offices and real estate multiple-listing services; verifying vacancies rarely presents a problem. The length of an interview will vary with the number and complexity of questions. The amount of time required to administer one question on household size and several questions on characteristic detail should average 10-15 minutes in a smooth-running interview. Large households and recall problems will extend interview length.

The number of interviews to be conducted in either the benchmark sample or an update sample will vary with the number of sample clusters, but the exact number of interviews can never be known in advance, because total households and occupied units are random variables in the sampling process. The number of sample clusters drawn will depend on both the unit cost of sampling and the predetermined level of statistical precision. The rules governing sample-size determination for a single-stage cluster scheme involving enumeration of sample units can provide general direction (Kish, 1965).

Another cost of fieldwork that frequently arises in cluster sampling is the cost of listing sample units. Since the population estimation procedure involves cluster enumeration rather than subsampling, the listing of units is really not necessary unless the user wants to maintain written records on the housing composition of sample address ranges. It is interesting to note that records maintained on sample housing units during the benchmark and update sampling operations can serve to disaggregate the ratio estimate of population change into separate estimates of change for the total number of housing units, the number of occupied units, and average household size. This information might be quite useful for certain planning and research applications.

The final category of expenditure is the cost of information processing. Sample questionnaires must be edited and coded, and coded responses must then be punched onto computer cards. Editing can be done on a rather limited scale, possibly by looking at every ninth or tenth questionnaire, unless interviewers express concern about the probable accuracy of certain responses. Coding is a mechanically simple process, especially for a relatively short and uncomplicated instrument, and interviewers might even be paid to do their own coding, unless other facilities are available. Punching coded responses on computer cards can be done for a nominal unit cost at almost any university computing center. If punching facilities are not available, the user may want to consider coding responses on optical scanning sheets. This method might even be less expensive on a per-unit basis than punched cards.

Once the sample questionnaires have been completely processed, the data set can be screened for potential problems.

Interviewer effects should be minimal, if they even exist, because the questions require no real interpretation on the part of the person conducting the interview. Response errors should also be minimal, since the respondent is reporting basic factual information of a generally nonsensitive nature. Coverage errors may pose a problem, however, because some persons will refuse to participate in the survey, and interviewers will not be able to locate others after a reasonable number of attempts. If coverage errors can be assumed to operate to the same degree in both the benchmark and update surveys, then the estimates of demographic change will not be affected. This assumption is probably warranted under most circumstances, although it is clearly a statistical convenience.

The remaining costs of information processing will cover the computer programming necessary to evaluate sample responses and prepare the final population estimates. These costs should be relatively small.

RECOMMENDATIONS

The population estimation procedure presented in this chapter should not be applied without question to just any metropolitan area. The procedure should generally be restricted to areas where (1) a cluster sampling frame can be constructed with relatively little investment, possibly using a GBF/DIME System, and (2) a longitudinal survey operation can be conducted without major logistical problems. For the most part, such restrictions are not so severe. The procedure should be capable of producing useful estimates for most metropolitan counties, minor civil divisions, and incorporated places. It should also work reasonably well for special administrative and statistical units, such as school districts and health service areas.

The accuracy of the survey estimation procedure will be strongly influenced by the homogeneity of the study area with respect to postcensal growth. The procedure cannot be expected to produce useful estimates for areas where growth during the postcensal period is highly unevenly distributed across primary sampling units. A cursory examination of equation 3, the expression for the sample variance of estimated total population, will verify this observation. A trend analysis of recent growth among units within the study area should provide some indication of the extent to which differential growth may affect estimator precision.

The survey approach to population estimation provides a unique opportunity to measure demographic change through direct observation. This opportunity is not without its price, however. Survey estimation is more expensive than other procedures that might be appropriate in a particular situation. Indeed, cost is the major reason most state and local governments restrict their use of sample surveys to situations involving legislative mandates, usually federal mandates, where survey expenditures can be charged to a federal contract.

The author can suggest two ways to reduce survey costs. First, the information produced by current population and housing surveys is almost always useful to more than one agency. To the extent that the information needs of a number of agencies are similar and can be satisfied by a survey of modest proportions, the total cost of survey work can be distributed over a broader budgetary base. While few agencies at the local level can afford to support a full-scale survey, most can contribute to a survey effort that will benefit all. Second, the effective cost of survey research can be significantly reduced by realizing that most surveys, particularly those containing current demographic information, have a reasonably good secondary market. This permits the total cost of survey work to be subsidized over time by the subsequent sale of sample estimates to groups not involved in the original survey effort. Other ways to reduce survey costs are certainly possible. Further improvements in the cost efficiency of survey research at state and local levels should stimulate greater interest in the use of sample surveys for planning and policy research.

96   Survey Approach

REFERENCES

COCHRAN, W. G. (1977) Sampling Techniques. New York: John Wiley.
KISH, L. (1965) Survey Sampling. New York: John Wiley.
MORRISON, P. (1971) Demographic Information for Cities: A Manual for Estimating and Projecting Local Population Characteristics. Report R-618-HUD. Santa Monica, CA: Rand Corporation.
SILVER, J. (1977) "The GBF/DIME system: development, design, and use." Presented at the 1977 Joint Annual Meeting of the American Society of Photogrammetry and the American Congress on Surveying and Mapping.
SPIEGELMAN, M. (1968) Introduction to Demography. Cambridge, MA: Harvard University Press.
U.S. Bureau of the Census (1978) The Current Population Survey: Design and Methodology. Technical Paper 40. Washington, DC: Government Printing Office.
——— (1977) Developmental Estimates of the Coverage of the Population of States in the 1970 Census. Current Population Reports, Series P-23, No. 65. Washington, DC: Government Printing Office.

8

Alternatives for Monitoring
Local Demographic Change

Peter A. Morrison

INTRODUCTION

In addressing ourselves to the purpose of this conference, which is to evaluate how the size and composition of small area populations can be estimated, it is helpful to begin with a list of the variables to be updated. These variables derive from the Mental Health Demographic Profile System (MHDPS) and fall into two categories of priority (see Goldsmith et al., 1975):

Highest priority:

   (1) size of total population
   (2) percentage black
   (3) age-sex composition of total population
   (4) age-sex composition of black population

Lesser priority:

   (5) size of low-income population
   (6) number of low-income blacks and/or principal minority population
   (7) percentage of household population that is primary individuals
   (8) percentage of black household population that is primary individuals

AUTHOR'S NOTE: Views expressed here are the author's own and are not necessarily shared by Rand or its research sponsors.

(9)   percentage of dwelling units that is single, detached
(10) percentage of black-occupied dwelling units that is single, detached

These variables are to be estimated for several kinds of areal units: aggregates of census tracts, minor civil divisions (MCDs), census county divisions (CCDs), and whole counties (Goldsmith and Unger, 1973). A variety of estimation techniques might be useful for this task. The choice among them, however, is far from straightforward and involves several criteria.

Part of the assignment is to consider the merits of one such technique—the survey approach to small area estimation as presented by Norfleet W. Rives, Jr. (this monograph). I shall do so from two perspectives: (1) from the perspective of a specific technique to be applied, where considerations of feasibility inevitably enter in, and (2) from an analytical perspective, where we can consider how the logic on which it is based might be extended. My conclusion, which I shall state at the outset, is that the procedure is noteworthy, not for its immediate feasibility, but because its underlying logic points toward a powerful strategy for monitoring local demographic change. Accordingly, I shall focus not only on the particulars of Rives' proposed estimation technique (e.g., where the approach might be applicable), but also on the general strategy it suggests and how its logic might be extended.

NATURE OF THE PROBLEM

As background for this inquiry, we need to view the estimation problem in broad perspective. Certain variables that have been measured by census enumeration have to be updated: the size of an area's total population and of specific subpopulations defined by age, sex, race, and so forth, within that total. Such updates serve several purposes.

First, such demographic information serves important planning purposes, our central concern here. A typical health program, for example, involves *facilities* that must be sized, and sites; a *program* that must be planned and once in operation, evaluated; and a *target population* whose prospective needs must be estimated.

Second, with the advent of revenue sharing and other programs that distribute federal largesse, localities have come to attach considerable importance to these estimates, particularly the population totals for small areas. The formulas for distributing this aid typically give weight to the number of inhabitants an area claims.

The MHDPS can potentially address both the planning and the distributional issues. With respect to planning, the system enables the delineation of residential areas with common social rank, lifestyle, ethnicity, and other related characteristics, and furnishes one of the necessary elements for estimating the health and related needs of the population of those areas. With respect to distribution, which is fundamentally a political matter, the MHDPS lends itself to developing comparative measures of need that provide an objective basis for informed decisions about allocating services to underserved areas. With an objective framework, politically charged questions of which areas merit more service can be negotiated on the basis of fact.

The need to update information, of course, is premised on the assumption that variables have undergone meaningful change since the last census enumeration—meaningful in a *planning* sense to those who seek to meet the needs of the ever-changing target populations, and in a *political sense* to those who may claim that they are (now) underserved.

Certain variables are virtually certain to change, such as total population size, or other absolute measures; others, such as the proportion who are elderly and other similar relative measures, may change so little that the change cannot even be detected.

ALTERNATIVE APPROACHES TO POSTCENSAL ESTIMATION

A variety of procedures can be used to update demographic variables for small areas. Most of us already are familiar with these procedures; the emphasis in this section will be on their underlying logic. For this purpose, the task of postcensal updating is something like estimating how many bricks lie behind the high fence of a brickyard, while one stands outside. The last inventory was in 1970, and yet we must estimate how many bricks there are now, and of what types. Strategies for doing so include:

(1) extrapolating the observed trend between two previous time points;

(2) compiling statistics on flows, e.g., the daily numbers of bricks trucked in and out;

(3) relying on indicators of activity, e.g., the comparative number of employees today versus 1970; and

(4) hiring a surveyor to measure the dimensions of the brick pile from the inside.

The corresponding approaches to postcensal estimation, of course, are *simple extrapolation, component analysis, analysis of symptomatic data,* and *direct surveying.* Some procedures may combine the logic of several of these approaches.

For the kinds of applications under consideration here, each approach has particular strengths and weaknesses. Drawing on two earlier documents (Morrison, 1971, 1977), let me quickly summarize them as a prelude to further discussion (see also Shryock et al., 1971; Pittenger, 1976; Irwin, 1978).

TREND POPULATION

The simplest but least satisfactory approach to postcensal estimation is to extrapolate a past trend in net change. Trend-based methods rest on the assumption that change follows a fixed trajectory that can be expressed mathematically or graphically. Although they are analytically crude, trend-based procedures often suffice for short time horizons and can be useful for updating variables quarterly or semiannually.

Applied to the long term, extrapolation is inadequate on two counts: (1) It does not distinguish analytically the different components of population change (fertility, mortality, inmigration, and outmigration); and (2) it presumes that those components will continue to yield an identical net effect as they interact over time. A further drawback of special concern for health planning is that simple extrapolation procedures ignore the important dimension of age composition, which can be expected to change in a "nonextrapolatable" way. Because simple trend extrapolation has limited utility in this case, no further discussion is devoted to it here.

COMPONENT ANALYSIS

Component analysis, which is the orthodox demographic approach to estimation, amounts to a more sophisticated form of extrapolation in which the observed effects of demographic processes are projected ahead. Explicit account is taken of the components of population change and their influence on population size and structure. Starting with the population distributed by age and sex, the population is "survived" ahead, according to a schedule of recorded or estimated vital events. Allowances are made for migration, either net or gross, on the basis of previously observed rates.

Given the salience of age composition to health planning, component analysis is the favored approach, assuming that the necessary data are available. It has certain limitations, however. Its logic is undermined where there is substantial population turnover through migration. This may be a particularly acute problem on the small area scale. Net migration gains or losses, of course, are only the surface ripples of powerful cross-currents that are continually recomposing a locality's population. Over only a few years, many of the original residents may depart and be replaced by newcomers, quite possibly with different survivorship characteristics (e.g., departing youth replaced by elderly retirees). With so many different people coming and going each year, it is not safe to assume that the population will consist of more or less the same people from the base year throughout the estimation period. Population turnover is generally more brisk the smaller the area under consideration; and even though the size of the population in a census tract may change little over the years, its membership may include only a few of the same people.

ANALYSIS OF SYMPTOMATIC DATA

A third approach relies on various types of symptomatic data that reflect the size and composition of an area's population. Such data may be records of *events* occurring regularly in a population (e.g., vital events, income tax returns, voter registration) or of population related *objects* and *services* (e.g., school attendance, occupied dwelling units, building permits, residential telephones, electric and water meters, motor vehicle licenses). The assumption here is that changes in the population's size will be reflected in these variables.

For counties, a wide variety of symptomatic measures are available for tracing population trends. Below the county scale, options are limited and differ from state to state. As a general rule, any data series is a potentially useful symptomatic measure if: (1) It is coded to relevant small area units (e.g., health districts within a city); (2) it contains relevant compositional distinctions (age, sex, race, income, welfare status, and the like); and (3) it is available on a regular and timely basis.

For many cities, vital statistics are the only series that fulfill these three conditions, pointing toward their use as symptomatic indicators. In one application of this approach, vital statistics proved to be useful for monitoring small area population changes in cities (Morrison and Relles, 1975).

Although vital events figure in both component and symptomatic approaches, they do so in fundamentally different ways. In component analysis, births and deaths are like bricks added and subtracted; in symptomatic analysis, they serve as observable indicators of an unobserved population, analogous to the number of brickyard employees.

In certain hybrid techniques, both component and symptomatic approaches are combined. For example, the component analysis logic may account for how births and deaths have modified a population through natural increase; the symptomatic logic may link changes in net migration to changes in school enrollment or out-of-state driver licenses.

Symptomatic analysis is vulnerable to two weaknesses. First, the sensitivity of most indicators is weakened by extraneous factors. The number of dwelling units in an area, for example, is sensitive to shifts in occupancy rates and average family size as well as to the population's changing size. Second, symptomatic data may be more sensitive to change at some ages than at others. For example, births are most closely reflective of the number of young adults, whereas deaths tend to reflect the number of elderly persons. Certain estimation techniques (e.g., the Bogue-Duncan Composite Method) take advantage of this fact by building on multiple symptomatic measures, each designed to gauge a particular age group within the population.

SURVEY APPROACHES

Approaches that rely directly on survey data defy simple generalization. The method proposed by Rives relies on direct observation to estimate population size and composition for administrative and statistical areas below the state level, e.g., counties, incorporated places, MCDs, school districts, and medical service areas. Essentially, it samples high-grade evidence of population change—glimpses into the brickyard—and uses this evidence (1) to evaluate the current worth of the most recent measure of a variable (which amounts to testing the null hypothesis that the variable is unchanged since it was last measured), and (2) assuming rejection of the null hypothesis, to reestimate the variable. This procedure is noteworthy for the strategy it suggests: namely, to regard the variable measured as being potentially out of date and, as necessary, to "buy" additional information with which it can be updated.

APPRAISING ALTERNATIVE APPROACHES

The logic of the approaches just described translates into various operational procedures that have to be implemented with data that may be imperfect and difficult to come by. A central interest lies in the population's social differentiation across small areas, because spatial aggregation tends to conceal important differentiations of special concern to health and other planners. A real scale, therefore, becomes a major consideration, since important features of such differentiation will be missed if the geographic unit adopted is too large. For example, a county with a rising percentage of population 65 and over may warrant the development of new facilities to service the needs of the elderly. The facilities may be underutilized, however, if they are not located near the concentrations of elderly persons. To have practical applicability, therefore, a method must be able to detect specific retirement communities within what may be a large and heterogeneous county.

Health planners inevitably face a tradeoff between the competing needs for more spatial resolution, which of course, restricts the choice of input data and may leave simple extrapolation as the only remaining option.

A second consideration here is that particular estimation methods perform better under some circumstances than others (Morrison, 1971; Voss and Kale, 1977; Isserman, 1977). Looked at another way, each method has distinctive vulnerabilities; there is no single "best" estimation method. Indeed, we are well advised to rely on a combination of different methods, since an average of several estimates, each arrived at through the application of different methods, tends to outperform any single method.

A third consideration, of course, is the budget constraint. Certain methods are several times more expensive to implement than others. Even if it yields demonstrably more accurate results, the more expensive procedure is not always feasible. As a practical matter, certain approaches become feasible only under the aegis of a federal or state agency that can muster the resources to coordinate the assembly of input data, calibration of methods, and evaluation of precision. (The Population Research Unit in California's State Department of Finance, and Wisconsin's State Population Estimation Unit, are two exemplary cases.) The budget constraint is a major consideration in evaluating survey approaches, which rank among the more expensive estimation methods. Inevitably, one must weigh the less expensive alternatives that are available.

Selecting the "best" estimation method, then, calls for considered judgment; it is not a simple matter of choosing between the Volkswagen and the Cadillac. To make such a judgment we must consider the spatial detail that is needed; whether the demographic setting is one of rapid change or relative stability; and the marginal cost one can afford to pay for improved accuracy.

With this background, we can now consider the survey-based procedure that Rives has proposed. This procedure exemplifies a general approach to updating that can be labeled "information buying," a strategy that entails monetary investments in information to resolve key uncertainties about the variables in question. Viewed in this light, at least three issues figure in an overall assessment of this method: (1) How else this information might be acquired; (2) the circumstances that would warrant such investment in information; and (3) how the technical implementation of this method might be improved.

My overall conclusion in light of these issues can be stated succinctly: The technique Rives has proposed is a sensible one that can complement other techniques that might be used, and is one that might be used, and is one that no reasonable person can quarrel with, *except* on grounds of cost. Because it is sure to be costly, though, the central considerations favoring adoption of this procedure are likely to be situational, not technical. Although it is not a procedure that recommends itself for widespread use, it may be well suited to certain types of settings. What is more important, I believe, is that the logic behind its use may have broader applicability as an information buying strategy, a point I shall explicate in the following section.

THE ROLE OF INFORMATION BUYING
IN MONITORING DEMOGRAPHIC CHANGE

The basic strategy suggested by Rives' survey-based method is to purchase information in stages. This logic is reflected in his approach, which entails determining first whether there has been any detectable change and then proceeding with actual estimation. Broadening this idea, consider the possibility of *monitoring* demographic processes more or less continuously. Conventional indicators of fertility and migration at the national and regional scale (from *Current Population Reports*) could be combined with indicators that signal noteworthy turning points in local level population dynamics. For example: (1) Do local fertility trends continue to parallel national trends? (2) Has the volume of net migration continued unchanged since it was last measured on the census? (3) Has the age-race composition of gross migration flows continued unchanged since the last census? Where our monitoring procedures do not detect any significant change, we are then justified in applying component analysis techniques, assuming the necessary data are available, or less sophisticated trend extrapolation methods.

Where change is apparent, the analyst will be in the market for more information, and a survey-based approach is one option for consideration. Other options should be explored, however. Are alternative, less costly sources of information available? Unlike a decade ago, a considerable amount of administrative by-product data is now available and lends itself to monitoring local demographic change, particularly at the county scale. This "free" information includes, for example:

- annual counts of elderly Social Security recipients by county, going back to the 1950s;[1]

- estimated gross migration flows into and out of revenue-sharing jurisdictions, based on a match of IRS records (These estimates were prepared in conjunction with the Census Bureau's preparation of population estimates for revenue sharing.);

- annual counts of welfare recipients;

- vital statistics for health areas within cities, widely available and potentially useful for symptomatic estimation techniques.

In addition to such administrative by-product data, large-scale surveys that furnish current information on specific places have become increasingly common in the 1970s. Most noteworthy, perhaps, are HUD's Annual Housing Surveys, conducted in several dozen SMSAs. These data can be disaggregated within each SMSA (e.g., by central-city and noncentral-city counties), making them potentially useful sources of information with which to contrast the health needs of such areas. Some of these SMSAs have been resurveyed at a second time point, making these data even more useful for monitoring postcensal demographic trends. Other surveys (e.g., the Survey of Income and Education) also may have applications here.

USING EXISTING DATA TO MONITOR LOCAL CHANGE: AN ILLUSTRATION

As an illustration of how administrative by-product data are useful for monitoring local demographic change, I shall outline some possibilities for monitoring changes in the distribution of elderly population at the county scale, using the first of the above data sources: the annual number of elderly Social Security recipients. The residential choices of older citizens have important implications for the localities in which they choose to settle. Because their service needs differ from those of other age groups, the elderly impose special service demands on the localities where they reside. Apart from the decennial census, however, there has been no straightforward procedure for monitoring the geographic redistribution of elderly citizens. Public agencies, especially those involved in health planning where lead times tend to be long, could benefit from current demographic information that enables them to foresee future service needs.

The *relative* share of elderly in an area can increase, irrespective of how frequently (or infrequently) the elderly population migrates. This point can be explained with reference to Table 8.1, which illustrates how counties can be classified by: (1) the net migration rate for the *total* (all ages) population, and (2) the ratio between the rates of elderly and total net migration.

The sign in each cell of Table 8.1 indicates, for the given configuration of rates, how the relative share of elderly persons in the population would change. The configurations of primary

TABLE 8.1   Analytical Typology

Ratio of Elderly to Total Net Migration Rates	Net migration rate, total population		
	Strongly Negative	Nominal	Strongly Positive
Well above 1.0	–	+ (recomposition)	+ (congregation)
Approximately 1.0	0	0	0
Well below 1.0	+ (accumulation)	–	–

+ denotes increasing share of elderly
– denotes declining share of elderly
0 denotes no change

interest in this study are the three cells marked with a "+," indicating an increasing concentration of the elderly.

The configuration labeled *accumulation* describes elderly concentration in an area that comes about through the departure of young and mobile residents and retention of elderly residents. As the population shrinks, the percentage of elderly rises. The configuration labeled *recomposition* describes a process of age-specific recomposition, which comes about when net migration flows in opposite directions at different ages: a net inflow of elderly people is offset by a net outflow at most other ages. A third configuration, labeled *congregation,* comes about when the county's population gains migrants of most or all ages, but the elderly inmigration rate exceeds the nonelderly rate.

Annual counts of elderly Social Security beneficiaries by county provide a basic symptomatic measure that closely reflects changes in the elderly population's distribution. Table 8.2 (drawn from an earlier pilot application to New York State) illustrates one procedure for identifying where New York State's elderly population is now disproportionately concentrated or becoming so. The "Index of Elderly Concentration" shown there is defined as a given county's share of all New York State beneficiaries, divided by the county's share of New York State population. By showing the elderly population per capita

TABLE 8.2   Concentration of New York State's Social Security
Beneficiaries 65 and Older, by County: 1969 and 1975

County	Concentration Index[a]		County	Concentration Index[a]	
	1969	1975		1969	1975
Albany	1.029	1.067	Niagara	0.920	0.972
Allegany	1.056	1.033	Oneida	1.048	1.068
Bronx	1.054	0.993	Onondaga	0.882	0.195
Broome	1.079	1.124	Ontario	1.069	1.000
Cattaraugus	1.170	1.132	Orange	1.016	0.973
Cayuga	1.098	1.104	Orleans	1.032	1.004
Chautauqua	1.269	1.273	Oswego	0.953	0.886
Chemung	1.103	1.115	Otsego	1.266	1.267
Chenango	1.019	1.111	Putnam	0.791	0.742
Clinton	0.778	0.697	Queens	1.049	1.072
Columbia	1.328	1.355	Rensselaer	1.076	1.064
Cortland	0.938	0.933	Richmond	0.827	0.818
Delaware	1.159	1.162	Rockland	0.597	0.665
Dutchess	0.904	0.912	St. Lawrence	0.934	0.917
Erie	0.933	0.970	Saratoga	0.745	0.744
Essex	1.138	1.249	Schenectady	1.256	1.254
Franklin	1.150	1.131	Schoharie	1.253	1.141
Fulton	1.317	1.260	Schuyler	0.959	0.927
Genesee	1.028	0.990	Seneca	0.978	0.943
Greene	1.574	1.528	Steuben	1.035	1.019
Hamilton	1.432	1.516	Suffolk	0.683	0.718
Herkimer	1.189	1.132	Sullivan	1.308	1.337
Jefferson	1.268	1.222	Tioga	0.777	0.795
Kings	1.084	1.052	Tomkins	0.722	0.727
Lewis	1.003	0.931	Ulster	1.156	1.107
Livingston	0.847	0.832	Warren	1.300	1.262
Madison	0.879	0.855	Washington	0.976	1.020
Monroe	0.940	0.951	Wayne	0.963	0.916
Montgomery	1.482	1.460	Westchester	0.994	1.035
Nassau	0.749	0.834	Wyoming	1.021	1.015
New York	1.292	1.230	Yates	1.371	1.344

a Index of elderly concentration defined as:

CI = [county's share of NYS beneficiaries 65+ in 1969 (or 1975)]

[county's share of NYS population in 1970 (or 1975)]

at two different time points, such an index enables us to identify counties with, for example, an uncommonly high concentration index (e.g., Greene); a concentration index that has increased over time (e.g., Hamilton); and so forth. Notice that changes in this index vary from county to county. Both Greene and Hamilton Counties have a relatively high concentration index, but it is rising in Hamilton and declining in Greene.

As this example suggests, there are inexpensive alternatives to direct surveys. Although these alternatives may never substitute for even a peek inside the brickyard, they can add to the analyst's store of evidence and may pinpoint specific places where a survey may be needed. Other sources of administrative by-product data merit careful scrutiny for such applications, for they may usefully complement the expensive survey approach, or at least identify the areas where a survey would pay the greatest dividends.

CONCLUSIONS

The survey approach to local population estimation, as exemplified in Rives' method, has obvious advantages: It furnishes high-grade evidence of population change and is adaptable to different local circumstances. Its principal drawback is its expense, which leads one to question whether such an approach can have widespread use. It may be more appropriate to regard such methods as one instrument in the analyst's tool kit, a specialized tool suited to uncommon circumstances.

More noteworthy, I believe, is the way in which Rives proposes to employ evidence. His proposed framework has a logic of its own that ought to guide the *use* of evidence (however acquired) for health applications. This aspect of his contribution, expanded to a broader scheme of continuous monitoring, merits further consideration and development.

NOTE

1. Because these data furnish a lengthy time series, they provide a potentially useful basis for developing estimation models based on a symptomatic logic. Additional unpublished data, I am told, furnish age-race details for elderly recipients.

REFERENCES

GOLDSMITH, H. F. and E. L. UNGER (1973) Social Area Analysis: Procedures and Illustrative Application Based Upon the Mental Health Demographic Profile System. U.S. Bureau of the Census, Census Tract Papers, Series GE40 No. 9, Social Indicators of Small Areas, Washington, DC: Government Printing Office.

GOLDSMITH, H. F. et al. (1975) "Demographic norms for metropolitan, nonmetropolitan, and rural counties." Mental Health Demographic Profile System, Working Paper No. 24, National Institute of Mental Health, Adelphi, Maryland.

IRWIN, R. (1978) "A cohort-universe net migration procedure for population estimates and projections by age." Presented at the Annual Southern Regional Demographic Group Meetings, San Antonio, Texas.

ISSERMAN, A. M. (1977) "The accuracy of population projections for subcounty areas." Journal of the American Institute of Planners, 43, 3: 247-259.

MORRISON, P. A. (1971) Demographic Information for Cities: A Manual for Estimating and Projecting Local Population Characteristics, R-618-HUD. Santa Monica, CA: Rand Corporation.

——— (1977) "Forecasting population of small areas: an overview," in Population Forecasting for Small Areas. Oakridge, TN: Oakridge Associated Universities.

——— and D. A. RELLES (1975) "A method for monitoring small area population changes in cities." Review of Public Data Use 3, 2: 10-15.

PITTENGER, D. B. (1976) Projecting State and Local Populations. Cambridge, MA: Ballinger.

SHYROCK, H. S., J. S. SIEGEL and Associates (1971) The Methods and Materials of Demography. U.S. Bureau of the Census. Washington, DC: U.S. Government Printing Office.

VOSS, P. R. and B. KALE (1977) "Small area population estimates in Wisconsin: examination of the relative accuracy of estimates derived from three symptomatic data files." CDE Working Paper No. 77-47, Center for Demography and Ecology, University of Wisconsin-Madison.

9

Evaluation and Synopsis

The Editors

OVERVIEW AND GENERAL EVALUATION

It was generally agreed that there were two major disadvantages to the "Rives Survey Method." In the first place, it requires a degree of foresight seldom exercised by those who will some day need or make population estimates. In the second place, it is very expensive. Offsetting these disadvantages is the advantage of obtaining more precise estimates of the total population along with estimates of population characteristics for small areas. Furthermore, a variant of this method could be adapted by the Bureau of the Census and tested as a way of improving current estimates.

Even if they were so farsighted, few users would be willing to bear the costs of two sets of interviews. Interviewing costs are very high and still climbing, especially when undertaken by professional survey organizations. The other costs, those associated with the choice of sampling units and the processing of data, are not prohibitive, but require skilled practitioners with knowledge of local areas. Regretfully, we must conclude that the Rives Survey Method in its complete form—two surveys of all sample sites, usually block faces, is unlikely to spread far from Delaware or be used by any but professors with a cadre of willing students. The exception to that statement is its possible use by the Bureau of the Census or other federal agencies with access to administrative records.

AREAS WHERE HIGH PRECISION MAY BE OBTAINED

The Rives Survey Method should provide high levels of precision where the dwelling unit structure of sample sites—the number and type of units as well as street patterns—remains relatively unchanged. However, in areas where streets and buildings have been reconstructed or demolished, it may not provide reasonable estimates.

In areas where dwelling unit structures change little, two types of development can occur between surveys. In the first, households or families remain in the areas and the population changes that occur are largely due to the aging of the population, including moving away of young adults at the usual ages of entering college, joining the labor force, or getting married. The other type of change, however, involves the replacement of a population with younger or different people, as when racial succession occurs or when families whose children have grown up are replaced by families with young children.

LIMITING SURVEYS

For areas with stable dwelling unit structure, costs should be reduced by limiting surveys to areas where a lack of population stability is to be expected, and using cheaper methods in areas thought to remain relatively stable. Some of the money saved by limiting surveys could be used to develop procedures for estimating the characteristics of areas where marked changes are likely to occur such as those with considerable demolition or construction. These are areas where surveys are most needed but also most difficult.

Each type of area—for example, stable population and housing structure or stable housing structure but unstable population—must be identified at the time of the census or the concomitant survey. Identification of areas where housing units change little but where population succession is likely are among those where the Rives Survey Method is the most appropriate. These can be identified in several ways. A method now appearing to show promise is simulation, and to that we may add precensal and postcensal monitoring.

SIMULATION

David L. Birch, whose procedures are described in a following chapter, has developed a model that has been successful in projecting population and other types of change for small areas. The model utilizes standard criteria but permits variations that are related to the history and geography of an area. For such models, the requisite data have been assembled for only a few cities, and it is still difficult and expensive to obtain them. For larger units, say counties, more data are routinely available. If counties can be used as the unit of estimation, much can now be done in the way of modeling or simulation. For smaller areas, tracts or MCDs, the requisite data are not widely available.

We can, however, specify some minimal elements for a simulation model. First is density—gross density, of course, and net density if possible. The latter, land exclusive of lakes, parks and such features, is the land available for erecting residential and industrial structures. There areas are likely to be developed if they are in favorable locations, along a major highway or adjacent to already built-up areas, while areas that are already occupied with sound buildings are not likely to experience marked change.

As already suggested, we have to consider the context of the area for which estimates are to be made. By context we mean the land use patterns and the characteristics of the population in surrounding areas. By studying these we may be able to estimate the likelihood of change and its direction for the area in question. Both deterioration and improvement are likely to spread from an area to its neighbors, and the characteristics of an area often give clues to the demographic and economic changes to be experienced by neighboring areas.

Homogeneous areas probably change less and in more predictable ways than heterogeneous areas. This consideration, along with density and context, should provide clues to the direction and extent of population and housing change. Unfortunately, existing models do not allow us to identify, for major segments of the nation, the areas that are most likely to change. To identify these we need both precensal and postcensal monitoring.

PRECENSUS MONITORING

Currently we lack procedures that would identify the small areas most likely to undergo different types of change at the time of the census. This information is, of course, necessary if we are to select sample areas with stable housing structures but changing population characteristics. True, administrative records can be used to identify areas that are changing prior to the census, but we do not know the degree to which such changes predict postcensal patterns. We can, however, use 1970 and 1980 census data together to single out areas that have undergone marked changes. We can then classify these by type of change and by characteristics at the beginning and end of the decade. An initial hypothesis therefore would be that areas with particular characteristics in 1980 would be the most likely to undergo marked change.

POSTCENSAL MONITORING

At present, postcensal monitoring appears to be a more reasonable way of reducing the costs of surveys made in the Rives Survey Method. While the usual block face survey would be necessary at the time of the census, other ways of estimating change for areas expected to experience little change could be employed instead of surveys. Existing records available from the Bureau of the Census could be used in monitoring. These include Internal Revenue Service records, welfare records, vital statistics, housing records, social security records, and even maps produced from satellites. Windshield surveys—simply driving by and noting evidence of change—can be useful.

ALTERNATIVE SURVEY PROCEDURES
TO THE RIVES METHOD

The postcensal sampling procedure, suggested for use with the Rives Survey Method, is doubtless the better way of cutting costs but it remains the most expensive. It still requires that all areas be surveyed at the time of the census, though a reduction could be made in the number of areas surveyed at the time estimates are to be made. A possible alternative procedure is to replace block faces as used in the present Rives Survey Method with areas that could be identified by latitude and longitude. Some GBF/DIME files contain such information. By monitoring changes within a representative sample of constant small areas, changes in population and housing structure could be detected. If administrative records were coded to latitude and longitude such a procedure could be used.

For example, suppose that IRS data were coded to longitude and latitude for the year in which a census occurs and for any other year. Estimates of housing and population change between these dates could then be made using a method similar to that of Rives'. The major cost would be the coding of addresses on IRS or other administrative records. Furthermore, this procedure would not require a sampling of selected geographic units at the time of the census, and could be undertaken years after the census or at any time the need for estimates is perceived.

SUMMARY

In summary, the Rives Survey Method or similar procedures require awareness of the need for estimates years before they are to be made and entail considerable costs. It is therefore unlikely that administrators in cities or municipalities will adopt this method. Thus the development of the Rives or similar methods must depend upon adoption by an existing department of the federal or state government that has a staff that can explore the possibilities and develop the procedures.

Part Five

Using Simulation Procedures

10

A Behavioral Model of
Neighborhood Change

David L. Birch

The Community Analysis Model was designed to estimate year-by-year changes in small areas—mostly census tracts—within a metropolitan area. In one mode, it projects into the future assuming no policy or program changes and no unusual events, such as wars or depressions. It can also be used to estimate how sensitive neighborhoods and groups of people are to public and private actions of various kinds—housing projects, new plant openings, or changes in the transportation system.

A continuing goal of our modeling work is the development of a general behavioral theory of neighborhood change. We have spent a great deal of time attempting to formulate general propositions that will work in any city rather than ad hoc relationships that must be recalibrated from place to place.

This chapter summarizes our basic approach, how we have implemented the model in six metropolitan areas, the effort and cost required to add an additional city, and future directions of the project. The model and its supporting software are described in considerable detail in a series of publications outlined in Appendix 10.1. One set of monographs describes the theoretical and empirical foundations of the model; another set provides technical details for users of the model.

THE SEARCH FOR GENERALITY

Even the most casual observer of cities notices that they are not identical. The buildings look different. The spatial layout is different. Some of the people look different. The terrain and vegetation and climate are different. These differences raise a question of generality. Can we expect to find general rules or laws that govern behavior and neighborhood change, or, like the alchemists, are we wasting our time in such a search and should we treat each city and each neighborhood as a special case? The answer seems closely tied to the level of detail at which we choose to describe the system under study. At one extreme, we could treat individuals as very large, complex objects governed by intricate brains composed of neurons made from atoms and molecules. At the other extreme, we could view entire census tracts as units of analysis, and search for general patterns of neighborhood change.

We know that atoms and neurons behave regularly from one place to the next wherever they are found. We have very little understanding of how they combine into functioning brains beyond the simpler operations associated with motor control and vision, but we observe that, in general, one brain seems to function much like the next.

It is when we come to whole individuals thinking and behaving that we begin to observe differences that become important in the understanding of neighborhood change. Without pretending to have any particular competence in psychology or psychiatry, we can postulate that the basic needs and drives for survival, security, comfort, affection, and so forth, are more or less universally shared throughout the human species, but that we begin to notice significant differences among nations regarding the ways in which these needs are converted into thoughts about how societies ought to be structured and about the nature of acceptable behavior by individuals. Call them ideologies, or value systems, or cultures, or whatever you please; it is quite clear that through some process that is little understood in its details, nations develop different shared beliefs about acceptable behavior that are manifested in their laws and constitutions and forms of government and customs, and that these beliefs define to a great extent what the individual may or may not do and still be considered a member-in-good-standing of the society.

In our own particular nation, the United States, we have placed relatively great weight on individual freedom and right of individuals to own and protect their property. This emphasis has led, in turn, to a structure of business enterprise and forms of governance that permit, and even encourage, physical and social mobility (we are the second most physically mobile nation in the world), diversity of land ownership and forms of development, the general acceptance of monetary gain as a measure of success, and the conversion of money into status symbols of one sort or another (houses, addresses, cars, appliances, and so on) as a means of demonstrating that success. We have also defined traditional roles for particular members of society (young people, men, women, the elderly, the poor) which, while not immutable, tend to govern behavior to a great extent.

Because of our own mobility and our media, and the corresponding mobility and media of other nations (at least in the western world), we would expect to find cultures or ideologies to be universally acknowledged (if not shared) throughout a single nation. We would thus expect, and all the interview data we have examined suggest, that the resulting behavior of the individual (after controlling for a relatively few obvious factors such as age and education and ethnic background) should be more or less the same everywhere within a nation. We would not expect, for example, that a resident of New Haven who moved to Houston would radically (or even significantly) alter his or her behavior as a result of the move. Such a person finds the same goods sold through the same kinds of stores, the same information flowing over the same media channels, the same textbooks in similar schools, the same kinds of job opportunities, and the same basic values and concepts of societal behavior. Were this not the case, our high degree of mobility would be enormously disruptive.

In view of this uniformity in individual values and behavior throughout a nation, we are left with the question: Why are cities so different? If all members of broadly defined groups in a nation behave in roughly the same way, following the same basic rules, why do cities within that nation vary so greatly? The answer, we have come to realize, lies not primarily in spatial variations in the rules governing individual behavior but in the circumstances in which that behavior takes place—the stage, if you will, on which the play is acted out. This situation is similar to many in the physical sciences where a general law (like the law of gravity) produces different results under different circumstances. A feather and a lead ball fall at greatly different rates in our atmosphere, for example, in apparent defiance of the law of gravity. The difference, of course, is attributable to the circumstances in which the objects find themselves (falling through air), not to a deficiency in the underlying rule governing their behavior. In different circumstances (on the moon, for example) both objects obey the law perfectly and fall at exactly the same rate.

Analogously, the differences in spatial form we observe from city to city are not attributable, for the most part, to differences in today's thinking or rules of behavior, but are due instead to the fact that different cities were built at different points in time, using different transportation and building technologies, different employment bases employing different mixes of people, who immigrated from different origins and organized themselves into different kinds of political jurisdictions. Also, of course, variations in terrain, topography, and vegetation play an important role.

This finding has an important implication in the search for generality. If we understand the rules governing individual behavior correctly, and if we can describe the circumstances in which individuals find themselves accurately and in enough of the proper detail, we should be able to explain and predict neighborhood change in any city within a single nation using the same model. The laws are the same, and if we can control for circumstances (like air resistance in the case of the feather and the ball), we should be able to make general predictions without recalibrating from place to place. In short, we should be able to find the equivalents of the gravitational constant that will work anywhere, assuming that we search at the right level for them. Figure 10.1 summarizes the situation as we now see it.

The converse, of course, is that the search for generality at the wrong level is futile. In particular, it appears futile to search (as this author has done on occasion) for a general pattern of neighborhood progression per se that will hold from city to city, since the circumstances vary so greatly from place to place. It is individual behavior, not neighborhood change, that generalizes across spatial boundaries.

THE COMMUNITY ANALYSIS MODEL

In search of the general, we decided explicitly to formulate our model in terms of individual behavior and to aggregate upward from that point. Working within a single nation, we expected to find (and found) considerable generality at the behavioral level, without having to explain behavior in terms of the thought processes and motivations causing it. The model thus takes the form of a series of decision rules that describe how different kinds of individuals "behave" in different roles. We sometimes call these individuals "actors" because we are primarily concerned with the actions they take in their various statuses and roles. A list of the actors and the actions simulated in the Community Analysis Model by each is presented in Table 10.1.

Viewed from the perspective of a mathematically inclined researcher engaged in model building, the list of actors and decisions appears long and practically unworkable. To anyone

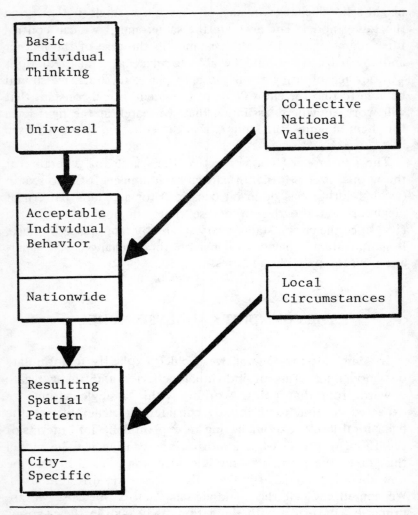

Figure 10.1   Levels of Generality

who has known neighborhood change, however, the list seems incomplete, leaving out many actors and actions that are experienced day in and day out in neighborhood life. This is a basic dilemma in any modeling effort. The list presented in Table 10.1 represents the minimum set of actors and decisions that,

TABLE 10.1 Major Actors and Decisions in the Community Analysis Model

Actor	Breakdown	Decision(s)
Household	Age by Ethnicity/Race by Education by Tenure by Price	1. To move within region 2. Choice of neighborhood 3. Choice of unit 4. Migrate in and out of region
Individual	Age by Ethnicity/Race by Education	1. Have children 2. Obtain education 3. Join workforce
Homeowner	Age by Ethnicity/Race by Education by Price	1. Setting selling price of home 2. Investing in home maintenance
Landlord	Rent Level	1. Setting rent levels on apartments 2. Investing or disinvesting in maintenance for apartments (including abandoning apartments)
Builder	Contract *vs.* Speculative Tenure and Price of Unit	1. Constructing single-family homes under contract 2. Constructing apartments under contract 3. Constructing single-family homes and apartments speculatively

(continued)

TABLE 10.1 Continued

Actor	Breakdown	Decision(s)
Lender		1. Lending for new construction and home mortgages
		2. Refusing to grant loans in certain neighborhoods
Insurer		1. Insuring homes and apartments
		2. Refusing to write insurance in certain neighborhoods
Zoning Board Member		1. Determining permissible land uses, granting variances
Employer	Major SIC Code Divisions	1. Location of a new firm
		2. Expansion of employment
		3. Relocation
		4. Contraction of employment
		5. Closing a firm's operations
School Superintendent		1. Modify school characteristics
Resident		1. Support (or not) existing school policies

based on our experience, explains most neighborhood change. We emphasize the "minimum" and "most." Any model is an abstraction, and the key decision is what to include and what to leave out. By working with this minimum set we feel it is possible to approach reality with enough accuracy for most planning purposes, and, at the same time, to live within tractable bounds mathematically and computationally.

The list includes actors from many different walks of life performing many different functions—moving, buying and selling real estate, building, locating and relocating businesses, zoning land, and running schools. The model consists of the behavioral rules that these actors follow in making each decision. Whenever possible, we have delved on a level lower, and attempted to explain the motivation behind the rule—why it works, if you will. But we make no pretense of basing the model on a theory of motivation. It is, instead, based on a theory of behavior and is invalid wherever the rules governing behavior are different, as in other nations.

Ideally, in such a behavioral model, each individual actor would make each decision each hour and its resulting spatial location would be known down to the parcel. In concept, there is no reason that this should not be done. In practice, maintaining such detail stretches computer capacity and cost beyond present limitations, and stretches existing data sources beyond their present resolution. Because of these limits, the researcher must decide whether to restrict the model to a relatively few individuals and parcels (as some have done) and abandon the reality of whole neighborhoods in whole cities, or to aggregate individuals and parcels and time to more manageable levels, sacrificing some of the micro-detail. In view of our interest in whole neighborhoods, we have followed this latter course. We have used census tracts, rather than parcels or street faces, as neighborhoods. We have lumped individuals into small, relatively homogeneous groups in each neighborhood and have described the probable behavior of the individuals in each group. And we have chosen to simulate decisions made each year rather than each hour or day or week or month, on the premise that most decisions affecting neighborhood change (moving, having children, building buildings, opening or closing businesses) are not made more than once a year by most individuals behaving in the system.

The Community Analysis Model operates by permitting each actor-group in each neighborhood to make the decisions for which rules are provided each year. The model begins with a known set of conditions and records changes in these conditions as a result of decisions made. If a household moves, for example, a housing unit in one neighborhood is vacated, another housing unit in another neighborhood is occupied, and the household and its members shift location from the first to the second neighborhood. Such changes are accumulated for as many years as the model's user desires. The output of the model is simply the revised set of conditions at the end of the last simulated year after all the decisions in the intervening years have been made and recorded.

Just as we must be parsimonious in our selection of actors and decisions, so must we consider carefully the way in which we describe the conditions or circumstances in which actors find themselves. If we are too limited in our description of the world, and restrict too severely what the actors can "know" about it, we cannot expect the actor's behavior to be realistic, nor, as we pointed out earlier, can we expect the rules governing their behavior to be general.

On the other hand, we cannot expect to include in our description of the world everything an actual person in that neighborhood might know. Such a person, for example, might know, for each structure on each parcel, when it was built, of what material it is built, by whom it was built, who has inhabited it since it was built, its color and shape, its size, its internal spatial layout, its history of maintenance, its landscaping and the condition of that landscaping over time, its cost, and so forth. And they would undoubtedly know precisely where it sits and hence how it relates to all these characteristics of all the surrounding parcels over time—be they businesses or residences or open spaces. Were computers larger and data available, and if we could show how such detailed information affected people's behavior, little argument could be mustered against maintaining such a detailed level of description. The reality, in the late 1970s, is that computers are not large enough, and, if they were, we do not generally have such measures of parcels in neighborhoods, and, if we did, we do not know how to relate them to behavior.

So we must strike a delicate balance. We must describe enough, and the right aspects of the world so that we capture the essence of what people know and respond to without overstepping the bounds of computer size and data availability and knowledge. Table 10.2 presents the results of striking such a balance in the Community Analysis Model. This table outlines the items the model keeps track of in each neighborhood each year—some 500-600 measures for each neighborhood. These measures, pieced together carefully over a period of time, have the following properties: (1) they can be obtained straightforwardly in most metropolitan areas in the United States (and have been obtained by us for six quite different areas); (2) they can be fitted onto any good-sized general-purpose computer; and (3) they offer enough of the right kind of detail to "drive" a generalized set of behavioral decision rules. In short, if you know the contents of the list of Table 10.2, the proposition is that you should be able to construct a model of neighborhood change that is based on generalized (rather than place-specified) behavior.

In one sense, the contents of the list in Table 10.2 are a major finding of the model. The list specifies the minimum set of circumstances we have found are necessary in order to predict neighborhood change with an accuracy acceptable for planning purposes. By implication, anything less than this will not suffice, and, while greater detail would be welcome and would further improve the generality and accuracy of the model, it is not essential in order to achieve "reasonable" accuracy. The list presupposes a set of decision rules that go hand in glove with it. These are described in detail in the publications mentioned in Appendix 10.1. It is also based on

TABLE 10.2   Main Items Kept Track of for Each Neighborhood

1. Number of households, by type of household, by type of housing unit
2. Number of people, by type
3. Number of households, by type
4. Average household income
5. Number of jobs, by type
6. Unemployment rate
7. Number of occupied housing units, by type
8. Number of vacancies, by type
9. Annual construction, by type of unit
10. Average condition of the housing stock
11. Annual maintenance of the housing stock
12. Abandonment of housing units, by type
13. Number of households dissolved (primarily through death) per year, by type of household head, by type of housing unit
14. Number of new households per year created through natural increase, by type
15. Number of households inmigrating per year, by type
16. Number of households outmigrating per year, by type
17. Number of local movers arriving, by type of household
18. Number of local movers leaving, by type of household
19. Excess demand for housing units per year, by type of household, by type of unit
20. Acres of land, by use
21. Quality of schools, by characteristic, by school
22. Maximum density at which buildings are permitted (through zoning)
23. Access time to every other neighborhood

For the Region as a Whole

1. Unemployment rate
2. Interest rates
3. Unemployment rate, by occupation
4. Unemployment rate, by industry
5. Unemployment rate, by type of person
6. Anything known at the neighborhood level

some concepts of "reasonable accuracy" and "generality," which will be discussed shortly. Within this context, however, it serves as a benchmark for comparing and contrasting different forms of analysis.

Having specified a set of actors and circumstances and decision rules, the designer of a model is left with a final problem: how to structure the sequence of events within any particular time period—a year in our case. In the actual world, the events described by the model are all going on at once, and, in most cases, without reference to each other. On a computer, we have no way of doing everything at once—things must proceed in sequence. The model builder must thus decide on the sequence in which events will be simulated, attempting, in the process, to roughly parallel any causal links or serialness found in the world. Figure 10.2 diagrams the flow through the Community Analysis Model within a particular year. The diagram reads from top to bottom and from left to right. It begins with employment changes that are related to natural increases and changes in the labor force. It then proceeds to simulate moving households and resulting changes in schools, housing markets, housing condition, land restrictions, and construction. The model itself consists of a series of submodels, each of which is called upon, in the sequence diagramed in Figure 10.2, to simulate the behavior of a single group of actors performing a function.

THE CONTEXT

This model was not built from scratch, of course. It is simply one of the most recent urban models so far evolved. To understand how it works, and its relationship to the reputed successes and failures of urban modeling generally, some comments on its "geneology" and evolution may be helpful. In developing the Community Analysis Model, we reviewed some 200 models of neighborhood evolution. The main line of formal model development has been the gravity model. Its fundamental premise is that people are highly sensitive to travel time and cost, and will

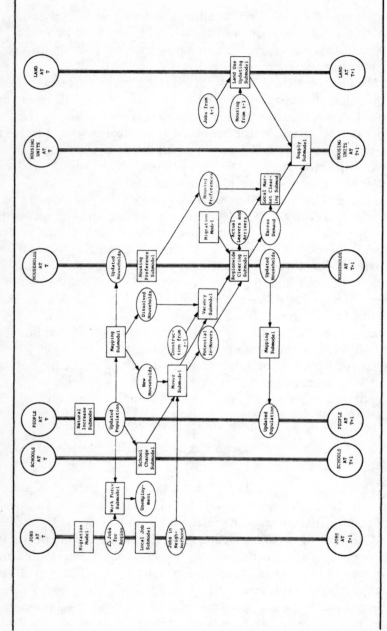

Figure 10.2 Summary of Flows Between Submodels and Resulting Changes in Memory

134

incur such costs only when a suitable residential location cannot be found near their place of work. The "gravity" label originated in the resemblance of the equation used to express cost-distance relationships to the gravity formula in physics. The original gravity model was developed in the late 1950s and early 1960s by researchers like Lowry and Alonso.

The basic gravity model has undergone numerous mutations, each attempting to enrich the theory by increasing the number of considerations entering into a household's choice of residence. One of these mutations is the National Bureau of Economic Research (NBER) model (see Ingram, 1972), which develops the supply side further and introduces a more sophisticated mechanism for representing the bargaining between buyers and sellers in the housing market. Building also on the transportation and land use focus of the gravity models have been several large efforts centered around particular regions—the Penn-Jersey Model (see Fagin, 1963) and the Susquehanna River Basin Model (see Hamilton, 1969), for example.

Taking another tack, Jay Forrester (1969) and his systems dynamics group at MIT have modeled urban evolution in terms of the balances between rates and flows of people and houses and jobs in a system of differential equations. The model has little or no spatial dimension and therefore takes no account of access or land use. Instead it focuses on aggregate relationships.

Not all social scientists who have conceptualized models of urban change have formulated them mathematically. In fact most have not. Their contributions have been important, however, and their starting points have tended to be quite different. Sociologists, for example, have usually conceptualized neighborhood change in terms of social status and changes in reputation over time. Modeling of this sort includes that by Fiery (1947), Suttles (1972), and Wolfe and LeBeaux (1967). Sociologists have added concreteness to their theory, not by writing equations for the most part, but by interviewing people to determine how they actually behave. Their emerging models differ significantly from those of the gravity school. For one thing, they find that the journey to work costs are important only if the journey is particularly long—40 minutes, according to Butler and Chapin (1969). Also, they find that people choose neighborhoods first—then find a unit in a satisfactory neighborhood. This is in direct contrast to the economists' focus on the housing unit as the primary basis for selection.

The geographers, meanwhile, tend to emphasize spatial patterns and the spatial organization of activities in their models. They are concerned with the rings and sectors and central places as the major describers of urban evolution and dynamics. Recently they have begun to relate space to human perception. Moore (1972) and Johnson (1972) have developed a concept of "mental maps"—maps of perception rather than real maps. They also relate behavior to these maps.

The Community Analysis Model embraces several of the traditions just mentioned. Structurally, it most strongly resembles the NBER model. Both models deal with the location of employment within the region. Both treat explicitly a stream of events that begins with movers leaving units, continues through vacancy accounting, a set of demand preferences for available units, a supply response for both existing stock and new construction, and both include a mechanism for matching supply and demand in the housing market.

Both models reject the concept of long-term equilibrium as an achievable state. That is, both are based on the understanding that rates of change in transportation, communication, food and energy costs, lifestyles, and housing preferences are at least as rapid as the ability of the region to respond—yielding cross-currents and an endless process of adaptation.

Where the Community Analysis Model and the NBER model differ basically is that the latter is built on the premise that economics alone holds the key to unraveling the urban puzzle. In developing our model, we rejected the notion that any single discipline holds the key. Our approach is that people are not predominantly economic people, or sociological people, or geographic people. Individuals' thought processes are not organized the way university departments are. They are "real people." When choosing a neighborhood to live in, they consider all kinds of things—cost, prestige, the view, their own self-images and lifestyles. They consider places they "know" a great deal more carefully than places they do not "know."

To complicate matters further, in our view, real people do not act like the near-perfect information processors and maximizers that much existing theory of urban modeling implies they are. Indeed, real people appear to be dominated by inertia—not action. They do not respond instantly and automatically to changes in price, or to class changes or to vacancies. Generally they put off moving as long as they can—particularly older households. Since landlords are also real people, sometimes they do not raise prices in the face of rising demand, as the maximizers would expect, for a variety of reasons. Builders, likewise real people, do not lay off workers and cut back construction as soon as vacancies and inventories rise. For a while at least, most of them think that "things will get better."

The net result for these different actors in an urban area can be far better described as "inertial adaptation" rather than optimization or maximization. Our model is based on a concept of "real people" engaged in adaptive behavior. It does not, of course, attempt to achieve complete behavioral description, but it is based on the recognition that people are influenced by a rich variety of information and stimuli, to which they respond in a complex way. We take the position that the economists, sociologists, and geographers are not wrong—only that they are partial and tend to emphasize just those aspects of behavior that fit nicely into their own theoretical rubrics. We have tried, instead, to draw on various viewpoints, confront them with the evidence available, and piece together descriptions of behavior that are consistent with that evidence.

IMPLEMENTATION

The model sits in a rich context of supporting routines that reduce, retrieve, and display data, as well as display corresponding model predictions. We have labeled the model and its supporting routines, "The Community Analysis System." It is diagramed in Figure 10.3.

The major task in developing the model for a new city is gathering the data to feed this system. Initial efforts at collecting data were very time consuming and expensive. For one thing, to validate the model, we had to go back at least as far as 1960, and machine readable data for 1960 are difficult to come by. Secondly, in many instances we extended our metropolitan areas beyond the tracted SMSA boundaries, forcing the collecting of MCD and CCD data for 1960, which was difficult to obtain. Finally, we required a number of data sets that cannot be derived from standard census products (e.g., employment by place of work, demolitions, public housing construction, travel times from neighborhood to neighborhood, and land use, to mention the most important).

Time, however, has been on our side. As the decade has progressed, most cities and local governments have automated most of their local administrative records for the 1970s and/or have joined state and federal programs that have had the same effect. Thus it is now usually possible to get good estimates locally of demolitions, public housing starts, and travel times, at low cost. We have ourselves developed a file of about 80 percent of the businesses in the United States (about 5.6 million business establishments with a time-series record spanning 1969, 1972, 1974, and 1976 for each establishment) making employment estimates by place of work relatively straightforward. When the 1980 Census arrives, permitting us to abandon 1960 as a starting point, and if we restrict ourselves to areas defined in the 1970 Census, we will be able to develop all the data required for the Community Analysis System in a relatively short time (three or four months) at low cost. Practically everything will be automated and derivable from conventional sources. The only exception will usually be land use, and many planning departments now maintain a progressive, automated land use accounting system. Thus, data gathering, which a few years ago was a costly and time-consuming affair, is becoming a relatively minor inconvenience. Its cost was once measured in

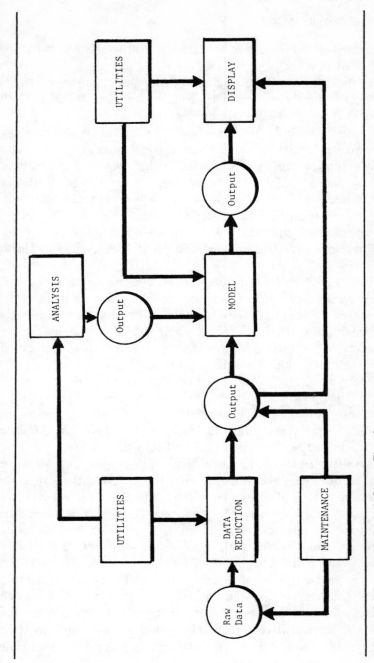

Figure 10.3 Community Analysis System Flowchart

139

hundreds of thousands of dollars but will shortly be measured in tens of thousands of dollars.

As the data come pouring in, and the model generates 30,000 or 40,000 numbers each year, a major problem is "seeing" the results. Our minds are simply not well enough equipped to integrate thousands of spatially arrayed numbers in slices over time to see a pattern or generate a conclusion. We have coped with this problem in several ways. First we have developed a display package that permits any user of the system to display any data item (from actual data sets or from model predictions) over time for any set of desired subareas. This display system is an interactive, English-speaking package that may be operated toll-free by any user in any one of 153 cities in the United States.

Building on this most detailed retrieval mechanism is a summary report generator that produces profiles of any neighborhood (or residential district, or community, or county) at five-year intervals. Included are items that most users seem to want to look at first. This package also operates interactively over the same telecommunications link.

The Center for Governmental Research in Rochester has taken the profile concept one step further by generating a hard-copy profile for each neighborhood in its region and publishing the results as a 256-page compendium. A sample of the Rochester report is included as Table 10.3.

Despite all efforts to summarize and simplify the presentation of numbers, we still find that users have difficulty seeing general patterns of change over time, and that we ourselves have the same problem in interpreting results. Switching to another medium, we have developed a means by which our model can communicate directly with a color television set, changing the color of each neighborhood as its characteristics change. Thus we can make "color movies" of an entire area over time to reveal the kinds of systematic patterns that get buried in the details of a tabular presentation. Using a laser-based video disk and a touch-sensitive screen, we will shortly be able to touch any neighborhood on the map and call up several hundred slides

TABLE 10.3: Sample Rochester Community Profile

CENTER FOR GOVERNMENTAL RESEARCH INC.
COMMUNITY ANALYSIS MODEL
MARCH 20, 1978

VARIABLES	1960		1970		1975		1977		1980		1985 DISTRICT COUNTY		PERCENT CHANGE NORTON MONROE		
	NO.	PCT.	NO.	PCT.	NO.	PCT.	NO.	PCT.	NO.	PCT.	NO.	PCT.	60-70	70-80	75-85
LAND AREA (ACRES)	2454	100.0	2454	100.0	2454	100.0	2454	100.0	2454	100.0	2454	100.0	.0	.0	.0
RESIDENTIAL	1085	44.2	1086	44.6	1096	44.6	1097	44.7	1098	44.8	1101	44.8	.1	1.1	.4
LIGHT MANUFACT.	20	.9	46	1.9	49	2.0	49	2.0	49	2.0	48	2.0	134.5	5.4	-2.4
HEAVY MANUFACT.	35	1.4	63	2.6	59	2.4	58	2.4	57	2.3	54	2.2	78.4	-10.0	-7.6
TRADE & COMMER.	138	5.6	113	4.6	116	4.7	120	4.9	128	5.2	138	5.6	-17.9	13.0	19.4
VACANT, EASY BLD.	168	6.9	49	2.0	30	1.2	27	1.1	19	.8	11	.5	-71.2	-60.0	-63.1
VACANT, HARD BLD.	114	4.6	22	.9	22	.9	21	.9	21	.9	19	.8	-81.1	-3.3	-10.2
UNAVAILABLE	895	36.5	1076	43.7	1083	44.2	1083	44.0	1083	44.1	1083	44.1	20.3	.6	.0
HSHLD POPULATION	42087	100.0	39481	100.0	37528	100.0	37284	100.0	36439	100.0	34497	100.0	-6.2	-7.7	-8.1
POP/RESID. ACRE	38.8	—	36.4	—	34.3	—	34.0	—	33.2	—	31.3	—	-6.3	-8.7	-8.5
UNDER 20 YRS OLD	12854	30.5	12120	30.7	10772	28.7	10663	28.6	10367	28.5	9718	28.2	-5.7	-14.5	-9.8
20 - 39 YRS OLD	9524	22.6	9284	23.5	8997	24.0	9118	24.5	9013	24.7	8619	25.0	-2.5	-2.9	-4.2
40 - 64 YRS OLD	13823	32.8	11747	29.8	11314	30.1	11168	30.0	10894	29.9	10313	29.9	-15.0	-7.3	-8.8
65 YRS & OLDER	5887	14.1	6331	16.0	6437	17.2	6332	16.9	6167	16.9	5849	16.9	7.5	-2.6	-9.1
NATIVE	33088	78.6	28317	71.7	26090	69.5	25454	68.3	24402	67.0	22984	66.6	-14.4	-13.8	-11.9
FOREIGN	8816	20.9	7848	19.9	7466	19.9	7269	19.5	6960	19.1	6319	18.3	-11.0	-11.3	-15.4
MINORITY	183	.5	3315	8.4	3968	10.6	4561	12.2	5076	13.9	5196	15.1	1711.5	53.1	30.9

(continued)

TABLE 10.3 Continued

L.T. H.S.EDUC.	33707	80.1	76.0	26288	70.0	25243	67.7	23519	64.5	20675	59.9	-10.9	-21.7	-21.4
H.S.EDUC.	6082	14.5	17.9	8326	22.2	8930	24.0	9605	26.4	10341	30.0	16.5	35.6	24.2
G.T. H.S.EDUC.	2299	5.4	6.1	2912	7.8	3111	8.3	3316	9.1	3483	10.1	3.3	39.6	19.6
UNEMPLOYMENT RATE	4.5	4.5	—	8.2	—	7.5	—	7.0	—	5.1	—	.0	54.5	-37.5
HOUSEHOLDS	13599	100.0	100.0	14260	100.0	14416	100.0	14461	100.0	14324	100.0	4.1	2.2	.4
POP/HOUSEHOLD	3.1	—	—	2.6	—	2.6	—	2.5	—	2.4	—	-9.9	-9.5	-8.6
HH 20-39 YRS	3671	27.0	28.3	3919	27.5	4065	28.2	4133	28.6	4156	29.0	9.2	3.1	6.0
HH 40-64 YRS	6761	49.7	44.9	6266	43.9	6274	43.5	6267	43.3	6177	43.1	-6.0	-1.4	-1.4
HH 65 & OLDER	3171	23.3	26.8	4076	28.6	4079	28.3	4059	28.1	3992	27.9	19.4	7.2	-2.1
HH NATIVE	9504	69.9	66.3	9197	64.5	9171	63.6	9043	62.5	8910	62.2	-1.3	-3.6	-3.1
HH FOREIGN	4045	29.7	29.0	4159	29.2	4140	28.7	4081	28.2	3873	27.0	1.4	-.5	-6.9
HH MINORITY	50	.4	4.7	906	6.3	1104	7.7	1339	9.3	1541	10.8	1224.0	102.3	70.1
HH LT H.S.EDUC.	10173	74.8	69.7	9040	63.4	8604	59.7	7923	54.8	6843	47.8	-3.0	-19.7	-24.3
HH = H.S.EDUC.	2336	17.2	21.6	3900	27.3	4376	30.4	4991	34.5	5826	40.7	30.7	63.4	49.4
HH GT H.S.EDUC.	1089	8.0	8.7	1325	9.3	1435	9.9	1545	10.7	1655	11.5	13.2	25.3	24.9
OWNERS	8968	65.9	59.3	8141	57.1	8012	55.6	7906	54.7	7667	53.5	-6.4	-5.9	-5.8
RENTERS	4631	34.1	40.7	6119	42.9	6404	44.4	6556	45.3	6656	46.5	24.2	13.9	8.8

or a short visual movie to reveal what the neighborhood looks like physically. We find that people gather enormous amounts of information from visual inspection (cracking paint, a broken door step, an abandoned car, a boarded-up store) that cannot be obtained from available statistical data. By interweaving a visual and statistical presentation, the analyst can arrive at an explanation of what is happening far more quickly and can present the results more effectively to policy makers.

At the moment, the video and video-disk outputs must be generated on a one-of-a-kind facility at MIT and exported to local areas on video cassettes. All those products will be produceable by off-the-shelf hardware shortly, however, and will be available to any local user who is interested.

EXPERIENCE TO DATE

The Community Analysis Model was initially developed in New Haven. As a second step, it was extended to Houston, and then to Dayton, Rochester, Worchester, and Charlotte. These cities were carefully selected to span a broad range of urban experience and, at the same time, be manageable from an analytical point of view.[1] A local planning agency has become a local partner in the project in each case, helping to provide data, validate results, and improve theory when errant results are obtained. Development of the Community Analysis Model has thus been very much a joint venture, with heavy local participation at each step. As a result, one year after the six models were completed, four of the six cities are now using the model and its supporting routines in their daily planning activities. They are making projections, evaluating government programs (housing, transportation, 208 water quality planning, and so on), examining the consequences of plant location, and assessing the consequences of neighborhood change for institutions providing services (banks, natural gas utilities, local governments, mental health agencies). The model has thus turned into a workhorse for those who invested initially in its development.

VALIDATION

The notion of generality, and the need for a general rather than an ad hoc model, raises the issue of validation. How are we to know that we have such a model? To what tests should we put it before we accept it as valid?

There are at least two kinds of validity: short-term and long-term. In the short run (10 to 15 years), we assume no major changes in technology (transportation, communications), the economy, or the culture (and resulting behavior), or at least we can assume that any such changes, if they do occur, are gradual and in a known direction. Under these circumstances, the model's equations should predict change reasonably well. In the longer run, all the equations must be treated as fluid. Technology does change, the mix in the economy (and what gets imported and exported) changes, as does our culture and the concepts of what is "normal" and acceptable and what is not. In this more fluid world, the concept of the word "valid" takes on a different meaning when referring to a model. To ascertain short-term validity, any model should pass at least three tests:

Test 1: It must produce checkable outputs—that is, outputs that can be measured for real places over real time intervals at the neighborhood level. We can only conjecture about a model that does not meet this test; we will never be certain that it behaves the way the world behaves. The fact that its results look "reasonable" to some chosen group of people gives us little comfort, since we never know whether it is the selection of the group rather than the model that determines validity.

Test 2: The model must work accurately in different cities with little or no recalibration. This test introduces two concepts: accuracy and calibration. Accuracy is obviously a relative concept. What may seem crude and approximate to one user may be more than enough for another. Furthermore, accuracy has a time dimension. Good accuracy for five years and rough accuracy for fifteen may be fine for an organization that can adapt to its environment over a five-year period, while the same model may be a poor basis for planning the construction of a facility whose capacity must be adequate, but not excessive, fifteen or twenty years from now.

Perhaps the best test of a model's short-term accuracy is its ability to replicate past events and circumstances over a reasonably long time period. If it captures all aspects of the neighborhoods being simulated over a 10- or 15-year period, then in the short-term future it should continue to perform reasonably well—subject to its passing a third test to be described shortly. Testing against likely futures is far less satisfactory, since it puts us back in the position of deciding who knows what the future holds.

There is an upper limit to the accuracy that any model can achieve. That limit is the measurement accuracy of the data. No measure of neighborhood conditions is perfect. It is always subject to measurement error. We are never certain about what happened in a neighborhood between two points in time. Rather, we know within certain limits (that are a result of the measurement system) what has taken place. The estimated population, for example, might be 4821 plus or minus 10 percent (or about 480). As the level of substantive and/or geographic detail increases, so does the error. We may know the total population of a city with a 1 or 2 percent error factor, while we might be off by as much as 25 percent in our estimate of the number of people who are old and are white in a neighborhood. Table 10.4 describes the estimates measurement accuracy for a few of the typical items that a neighborhood model should predict well.[2] Average differences between model predictions and estimated actual circumstances greater than those presented in Table 10.5 measure the degree of accuracy of a model.

Many model builders strive to minimize error by recalibrating their model for each new city. Calibration is the process by which the parameters[3] describing an equation in a model are adjusted to make the model work more accurately. Such calibration can be done by hand, guessing which values will work

TABLE 10.4   Average Percentage Error in Measurements of Population, Households, Housing Units, and Employment for Census Years

| | Population, Households, and Housing Units | | |
	Region	County	Neighborhood
Totals	± 1%	± 3%	± 5%
Marginals	± 2%	± 5%	± 9%
	Employment		
	Region	District	
Totals	± 1%	± 7%	
Marginals	± 5%	± 15%	

better, or it can be done by using any one of the several automated processes.

While the designers of the Community Analysis Model have not been able to avoid calibration completely when shifting from city to city, we treat the need to recalibrate as a measure of the weakness of our model and not as an assumed necessity of model building. The need to recalibrate implies a lack of generality. No one recalibrates the law of gravity each time it is used. The law works everywhere. It is a general law. If we are to feel comfortable in our understanding of neighborhood change, that understanding must be based on general, not ad hoc relationships and laws, and models based on such laws should require no recalibration of parameters from city to city. The same parameters, like the gravitational constant, should work everywhere. Our second short-term test asserts, therefore, that a model should work with the degree of accuracy desired by the user *and* that it requires little or no recalibration in the process of being applied to that user's situation. To the extent that it falls short of this test (as all existing models to varying extents do), it should be treated with suspicion.

The accuracy test for longer-term use of a model is more difficult to specify with confidence. Since we do not know how

TABLE 10.5   Average Percentage Error in Projections of 1970
Households from a 1960 Base by Area

Area	Level of Detail	Geographic Disaggregation:		
		Region	County	Neighborhood
New Haven	Totals	.025	.025	.071
	Marginals	.025	.025	.143
Worchester	Totals	.039	.039	.051
	Marginals	.064	.064	.126
Dayton	Totals	.003	.012	.081
	Marginals	.014	.042	.144
Rochester	Totals	.002	.017	.059
	Marginals	.007	.024	.122
Charlotte	Totals	.001	.006	.054
	Marginals	.026	.058	.139
Houston	Totals	.005	.037	.101
	Marginals	.006	.051	.198

future behavior will differ from behavior in the past, we cannot
use replication of past events as a test. The usual procedure
under these circumstances is to vary the parameters that the
model builder expects may vary in the future (like fertility rates
or access time or differential economic growth rates) and see if
the model responds in a reasonable way to such variations. All
such tests hinge on this fuzzy concept of "reasonableness," but
at least they isolate obviously errant behavior caused by a set of
conditions that were not considered when the model was
formulated. As such they serve a very useful purpose.

Test 3: The microparts of a model must stand empirical tests
well. It is unlikely, but possible, that a model could replicate
past history in many respects simultaneously (even without
major recalibration) and still be based on spurious assumptions
about individual behavior. The model could, in some sense,
"luck out" because the assumptions were related to, but not
based on, the underlying causality.

This third test cannot, in general, be carried out directly with
the model. Each behavioral assumption must be checked against

information about individual behavior (e.g., surveys, census summary tapes, directories) to make certain that individuals—observed as individuals and not in aggregate—follow the rules we have assumed for them. If they do not, and if the model is merely "lucky," its luck will eventually run out. Its users should not be the victims of this unfortunate occurrence.

The publications mentioned in Appendix 10.1 describe in some detail the extent to which the Community Analysis Model meets these three rather stiff tests of performance. In summary, it produces verifiable output in large quantity, and when checked against actual neighborhood experience, the accuracy is "reasonable" for most planning purposes. Table 10.5 presents typical accuracy figures for households for each of the present six cities. The model does require a modest amount of recalibration from place to place in order to achieve this accuracy, but only a modest amount. Approximately 90 percent of its parameters are the same for all cities. And its assumptions are consistent with, and whenever possible, derived from records of actual individual behavior recorded in interviews and directories and other sources of individual records. The need for any recalibration to achieve these results is, of course, bothersome to us, and suggests that a good deal of work remains before we can assert that we have a set of general laws governing neighborhood behavior. Still, the results do bring to the planner a tool with which he or she can make relatively short-term projections with confidence and can test policies that are not bizarre by historical standards.

FUTURE DIRECTIONS

Future work on the Community Analysis Model can be broken into three logical categories: (1) better theory, (2) better mechanisms for updating theory as new data become available, and (3) application to new substantive and/or geographical areas.

BETTER THEORY

While the search for better theory is never-ending, our experience with six cities gives us many insights into which parts of the model are general and which are not and hence need more work. In particular, every time we have to recalibrate a parameter from city to city we know we have an ad hoc, and not a general, relationship.

Areas in which we plan to work hardest on theory development include residential location, location of newly forming businesses, real estate pricing policies, and the processes by which a few carefully selected neighborhoods are revitalized in the midst of general decline. This list is not meant to suggest that other segments of the theory are perfect. Quite the contrary, they all could use several person-years of work. The list simply reflects our priorities at the moment, given our experience in the six cities we have worked with thus far.

UPDATING

A great help to modeling work such as our own has been the increasing availability of local data by neighborhood during intercensal years. Using combinations of surveys, administrative records, address matching, and state and federal data collection programs, local agencies are beginning to compile annual estimates of population (occasionally by age or race), housing stock, housing starts and demolitions, employment, and so forth, by neighborhood. Such data offer the modelers an opportunity to test parts of their theories on a continuing basis rather than once every ten years. While an obvious benefit, the use of such data also poses several problems. For one thing, they are rarely as accurate as the census figures. We need a way of deciding whether the data or the model is wrong. Also, the data are almost always partial. Rarely do they cover all neighborhoods in a region, or all aspects of a particular substantive area. Estimates of total population for example, or, if you are lucky, population by race or age, are frequently all that is known about population.

The challenge is to extract the information contained in these scraps of evidence and to use it wisely in updating our theories of behavior. If, for example, current data tell us that outlying areas are growing far more rapidly than they did through 1970, we must figure out some way of revising our theory of residential preference without knowing precisely who is living out there, or where they are being employed. Frequently, the way out of the puzzle is to conduct a highly targeted survey of households or employers to obtain the answer. In other cases, simply reflecting a recent change in the transportation network in travel times will do the job. In many situations, however, a survey is impractical, and we must be far more subtle in diagnosing which part of our theory is no longer realistic. We are now hard at work devising mechanisms to facilitate such a diagnosis. It will permit us to capitalize upon annual data series as they emerge.

NEW APPLICATIONS

Having already related our findings to natural gas consumption, banking habits, and a town's fiscal condition, we know that the model's outputs can be useful for practical planning purposes. We are now in the process of assessing the consequences of rising energy costs on transportation, and would like to examine more general effects of higher prices for energy. We are interested in the effects of decline on the fiscal management of cities, and would like to build on our work with one town to understand the far more complex problems of a large city. We are also interested in human service delivery. A group in Rochester, for example, is beginning to think about how to relate its detailed records on mental health to changes in neighborhoods and, as a result, be able to anticipate future demand for mental health services.

We have reached the point where we would like to extend our approach to other areas. As the cost of data gathering continues to drop, starting up in new regions becomes relatively inexpensive. We are now holding discussions with planners in several different areas, and hope, within a year or so, to be developing data and models for new places.

IN CONCLUSION

From a theoretical point of view, perhaps our major conclusion is that studies and predictors of neighborhood change must turn to the behavior of individuals if they are to find general explanations for what is taking place. There is no generality at the neighborhood (census tract) level or higher. Arbitrarily defined collections of people and houses and businesses make up these higher levels of aggregation whose characteristics can be changed by changing boundaries. But there do appear to be general rules governing the behavior of individual actors, given some knowledge of the local context. If we are to develop a general model that does not have to be recalibrated from city to city, it must be a model, at the least, of individual behavior, and perhaps of human motivation, and not of neighborhood change per se.

From a practical point of view, we have identified a set of actors and a set of neighborhood descriptors that, in combination, permit us to predict neighborhood change, with tolerable accuracy, for a diverse set of cities. While not totally general by any stretch of the imagination, our model is approaching generality, with about 90 percent of its parameters being the same from area to area.

As local data series and the 1980 Census become available, the cost of creating the necessary data bases for validation become quite reasonable. Practically all the data reduction now proceeds in an automated fashion from standard or nearly standard sources. By restricting our areas to those defined as census tracts and/or MCDs or CCDs, by using the 1970s as our validation period, and by capitalizing on recent advances in computer technology, we can bring the cost of getting started within the means of almost any local planning agency that is willing to make the effort to learn something new and to invest minimally in local data collection.

The problems we face now increasingly require more thought, not more data or bigger computers. We are finding that a model operating in the midst of a reasonably complete data set and an active and enthusiastic planning agency is one of the better ways to generate insights into how neighborhoods change.

NOTES

1. For a detailed description of the city selection process, see a report to HUD entitled, "City Selection for the Joint Center Study of Neighborhood Evolution and Decline." (MIT-Harvard Joint Center for Urban Studies, 1976).

2. Table 11.3 refers to different levels of geography, including districts (which are aggregations of neighborhoods), as well as the total region. Also, it refers to "marginals" in defining substantive detail. A marginal is the one-way breakdown of some item (like population) that is found at the margin of a two- or three-way table describing the population in joint terms. In the following example:

		Age			
		0-20	20-40	40+	Total
	White	100	50	40	190
Race	Nonwhite	50	30	10	90
	Total	150	80	50	

The items in the cells of the table, taken together, constitute the joint distribution, and the age and racial breakdown at the edge of the table are marginal distributions, or marginals.

3. For those with little or no mathematical background, a parameter is a number which is part of an equation and which can be varied to change the values the equation produces without changing the general shape of the equation. The equation for a straight line, for example, is:

$$y = a + bx$$

where a is the point at which the line crosses the y-axis, b is the slope of the line, x is a point along the x-axis, and y is the corresponding point along the y axis. a and b are parameters. If either is varied, the equation still represents a straight line, but different y's are produced for any particular set of x's. Models are simply interrelated groups of such equations. Varying the parameters varies the predictions the model produces.

REFERENCES

ALONSO, W. (1964) Location and Land Use. Cambridge, MA: Harvard University Press.

BUTLER, E.W.F. and S. CHAPIN (1969) Moving Behavior and Residential Choice. Highway Research Board. Washington, DC: U.S. Government Printing Office.

FAGIN, H. (1963) "The Penn-Jersey transportation study: the launching of a permanent regional planning process." Journal of the American Institute of Planners, February.

FIREY, W. (1947) Land Use in Central Boston. Cambridge, MA: Harvard University Press.

FORRESTER, J. W. (1969) Urban Dynamics. Cambridge, MA: MIT Press.

HAMILTON, H. R. et al. (1969) Systems Simulation for Regional Analysis: An Application to River-Basin Planning. Cambridge, MA: MIT Press.

INGRAM, G. K., J. F. KAIN, and J. R. GINN (1972) The Detroit Prototype of the NBER Urban Simulation Model. New York: National Bureau of Economic Research.

JOHNSTON, R. J. (1972) "Activity spaces and residential preferences: some tests of the hypothesis of sectoral mental maps. Economic Geography 48 (April).

LOWRY, I. S. (1964) A Model of Metropolis. Santa Monica, CA: Rand Corporation.

MOORE, E. G. (1972) Residential Mobility in the City. Washington, DC: Association of American Geographers.

SUTTLES, G. D. (1972) The Social Construction of Communities. Chicago: University of Chicago Press.

WOLF, E. and C. LeBEAUX (1967) "Class and race in the changing city: searching for new approaches to old problems," in L. F. Schnore and H. Fagin (eds.) Urban Research and Policy Planning. Beverly Hills, CA: Sage Publications.

APPENDIX 10.1

RECENT PUBLICATIONS RELATED TO THE NEIGHBORHOOD EVOLUTION AND DECLINE PROJECT

Models of Neighborhood Evolution—Birch, Atkinson, Coleman, Parsons, Rosen and Solomon, November 1974, 265 pages. (A review of some 200 models of neighborhood change, summarizing their explicit or implicit assumptions about individual behavior.)

The Behavioral Foundations of Neighborhood Change—Birch, Brown, Coleman, DaLomba, Parsons, Sharpe, and Weber, March 1977, 205 pages. (A summary of the major findings emerging from our analysis of survey results and other extensive files on individuals, households, and businesses. The supporting evidence on which the model's theories are based.)

The Community Analysis Model: An Overview—Birch, Brown, Coleman, DaLomba, Parsons, Sharpe, and Weber, March 1977, 31 pages. (A brief, nontechnical overview of the Community Analysis Model.)

A Behavioral Model of Neighborhood Change—Birch, Brown, Coleman, DeLomba, Parsons, Sharpe, and Weber, March 1977, 215 pages. (A nontechnical description of the theories of individual behavior on which the Community Analysis Model is based. Organized to parallel the model's structure.)

The Community Analysis Model—Birch, Brown, Coleman, DaLomba, Parsons, Sharpe, and Weber, March 1977, 325 pages. (A verbal and mathematical description of the Community Analysis Model.)

The Costs of Growth: Revenue and Expenditure Implications of Suburban Town Development—Allaman, January 1975, 286 pages. (Describes a method for predicting school enrollments, line items in a community's budget, and the tax rate on a year-by-year basis using the results of the Community Analysis Model.)

A Computer-Based Forecasting Model for Use in a Natural Gas Utility—Stack, October 1974, 144 pages. (Describes a method for forecasting residential energy consumption by fuel type by use, based on results from the Community Analysis Model. Developed in New Haven for use by a local gas utility in planning for future demand.)

User's Manual for the Community Analysis Model. Volume I: Technical Description—Weber, Parsons, and Birch, September 1977, 330 pages.

User's Manual for the Community Analysis Model. Volume II: Fortran Code—Weber, Parsons, and Birch, September 1977, 473 pages.

User's Manual for the Community Analysis Model. Volume III: Data Files—Weber, Parsons, and Birch, September 1977, 254 pages.

11

Assessing the Community
Analysis Model

Peter K. Francese

There are fundamentally two types of small area demographic estimates (or projections). The first are local estimates usually generated by an individual city, county, or regional planning organization and used almost exclusively for solving local problems or for local grant applications. The second are estimates produced by a single national organization for many metropolitan (or nonmetropolitan) areas at once.

Nationally produced estimates are used to evaluate neighborhoods or other parts of municipalities for the possible location of a retail store or, less frequently, a federal project. Dr. Birch's Community Analysis Model is clearly a local type that requires the participation of a local community organization, like a county planning department. While his model is conceptually and functionally sound at that level, it is important to recognize that it probably cannot be used for nationally produced small area estimates. The very elements that make the model work so well at the local level prohibit its application anywhere else. There are simply too many data elements, like building permits, that are required from local sources. Neither this nor the fact that the model requires "recalibration" from city to city should be taken as a weakness. Communities desperately need tools to help them evaluate local situations and deal with complex problems in a way that makes best use of their own locally gathered information.

Furthermore, the model produces a wealth of detail only dreamed of by producers of national estimates. Also, this locally maintained model should produce more accurate small area estimates and projections than any national model. There is, of course, a price for this. Dr. Birch measures the cost of data gathering in tens of thousands of dollars; the maintenance of the model and analysis of the results will add thousands more. This is still a bargain when you consider than even a modest size community of 40,000 spends tens of millions of dollars a year in police, fire, education, sanitation, and other municipal services.

Estimates developed by national organizations cost much less per community, and generally produce less accurate results, but their usual purpose does not require more precision. An evaluation of a local market for a franchise operation rarely costs more than a few hundred dollars and is sometimes used merely to justify an already chosen site. Just as preconceived notions affect national estimates, politics can affect local estimates. I have seen census tract population estimates for a major American city that were "controlled" so that all census tracts either grew or stayed the same—no declines were permitted. Presumably a more sophisticated model operated by competent professionals minimizes the chance of finding such biased numbers.

There has been an interesting side benefit to Dr. Birch's work. In trying to make some sense out of the thousands of numbers both going in and coming out of the Community Analysis Model, he has developed a very elegant display system. Many a complex computer model has been buried by its own piles of printout because managers who are the ultimate users of the information will simply not pay attention to unrefined data.

The color graphics on an old familiar television screen are what will "sell" the model to those who have to pay for it, and will assure its continued use in the decision process. It may seem like window dressing to some, but an attractive display system is just as essential to a complex behavioral model as are regression equations.

My final comments concern the data items that must be gathered for each neighborhood. A number of these items would appear to rely on a complete and accurate address coding guide, which may not exist for certain communities. Also, a few of the items (like annual migration) are particularly difficult to obtain accurately at the tract level. Lastly, one or two items, such as quality of schools, involve value judgments that will certainly vary from place to place. I suspect that these problems with gathering and tabulating the input data is what causes the model to require "calibration."

In general, I found Dr. Birch's Community Analysis Model to be well thought out and creatively implemented. While its complexity may prevent its universal application, the model makes important contributions to local data analysis techniques and estimates methodology.

12

Evaluation and Synopsis

The Editors

COMPLEMENTARITY OF PROCEDURES

The Birch method of estimating population for small areas is not a substitute for methods now used nationally. Nationally based estimates, like those made by the Bureau of the Census, are based upon standard data sets that are uniform for all areas for which estimates are made—administrative records procedures based on IRS returns, for example. They do not provide detailed population characteristics (e.g., age-sex by race) for small areas. Moreover, while generally satisfactory for estimating total population or per capita income, particularly for large areas, they can be far off for some characteristics of areas, and, consequently, must be corrected by using information that is locally available. The Birch method, a simulation method, is very different. It uses more sets of data, requires specific knowledge of the local area, and involves complex software, but provides for small area detailed estimates of population characteristics as well as estimates of total population.

These two approaches complement each other. The Bureau of the Census makes estimates for small towns and counties as well as for states and large cities. There can be no adjustment for departures from the general model except in response to local officials who object to the estimates and propose improvements that they can justify. Birch, however, focuses the efforts of highly trained people upon a single city and develops patterns of neighborhood change that are generally similar from city to city, but that are affected by conditions specific to the city under consideration.

Given the number of localities covered, the Bureau of the Census' method is cheap and makes little demand for skilled person-power. The $400,000 or so it takes to process the IRS returns is not much, given the 40,000 or more estimates that are made. Furthermore, this is a cost that could be reduced if changes were made in the way data are recorded and in the hardware and software with which they are processed. Thus, while the Census Bureau spends rather little per estimate, the Birch procedure requires a considerable outlay. Initially, the cost of developing the model in a given city was very high—the cost might be well over $400,000. However, Birch notes that the cost has been radically reduced. What previously cost $700 may now cost only about $4.00. The difference in cost is that the model is already developed and easily transportable from one location to another provided the location has the necessary data.

The Birch model has been used successfully for several cities, and appears to be valuable for many types of planning or research. It is designed as a general estimation model with small error, for use over long periods of time, past and future. The expectation for the model is that it will provide estimates to be used in short-term assessments of service needs as well as estimates of the long-term use of structures such as school buildings. With recalibration, the model appears to have this capacity; thus, when 1970 estimates based on 1960 and interim data were checked against 1970 census data, error levels of less than 6 or 7 percent were observed for neighborhoods. Moreover, Birch feels that when the general model has been validated, it may not be necessary to recalibrate the model in each new city. Currently, some recalibration of the model is required. Rather than a problem of generalization, some persons considered this to be one of the great advantages of the model. It is advantageous to have a model that can be easily adjusted to improve the fit between estimates and observed data and to take local peculiarities into account.

Though the Birch model has so far been used only for cities, it can be used for states with counties or other subareas substituting for neighborhoods used in studying cities. Within the states, much data are available for counties and municipalities, and one can imagine that in the future each state and each metropolis will make use of models such as those developed by Birch and his associates, both as an aid to examining the past and as a way of perceiving and preparing for the future. This presumes, of course, the development of relatively cheap computers with large memories and well-developed software, the availability of adequately trained technicians, and—more difficult to come by—the awareness of officials and planners of the possibilities now available. In this regard, the computer graphics that have been developed for the Birch model are important in making the results intelligible to the uninitiated.

ACTORS RATHER THAN AREAS AS OBSERVATIONAL CATEGORIES

Most of the current methods of making population estimates are based on typologies for models that use areas as the unit of observation. Since these models assume that similar types of areas change in similar ways, the decision-making processes of the residents of areas need not be considered, for they are adequately represented in small area characteristics. At the local level such models appear to account for something like 70 percent of the variation among areas over the short run, though in the long run the errors may be much higher. David Birch takes a different position. He asserts that if estimates are to be made for small areas, consideration must be given to the processes that generate the changes within. He attempts to do so by focusing attention on the individual, or, in his terms, the actor. The assumption is that changing population characteristics result from individual actions which, like the molecules in a

Brownian movement, seem random, but nevertheless conform in the aggregate to general, abstract rules. These rules may be derived empirically or by theory, and after checking by systemic observation, can be expressed in terms of probability distributions. Implicitly, the general rules apply across time and space. Given knowledge of such behavior, appropriately operationalized, it becomes a simple task to estimate population changes within an area.

Determining the ways in which actors should be classified in order to assess collective behavior is no easy task. Age, sex, ethnicity, household, and family status are obvious considerations, as are education and income. The problem is to reduce the many factors that affect individual decisions into a set small enough to be manipulated but adequate enough for determining the changes in population size and characteristics that spring from the decisions of individuals. Considerable work still remains before the best general set of causative dimensions is identified.

There is the question as to whether actors in different environments (neighborhoods, cities, regions) behave in roughly the same way given similar stimuli. This is a problem—the importance of individuals and their social context—that has long occupied epidemiologists and ecologists. Birch, in his theoretical statement, takes the position that knowledge about actors is the key to estimation; accordingly, given general knowledge of the behavior of actors, the specific social context should have little independent effect on behavior. Other social scientists assert that the social context of an actor has consequences for behavior that cannot be accounted for even if one were given complete knowledge of actors. Thus, they expect that at different times, similar people (actors) react in different ways, reflecting the variations in social, economic, and environmental conditions that may be short- or long-term. The effects of place are complex, representing as they do the combined pressures of national and local social environments. Interwoven into the racial context are the problems occasioned by the necessary combination of age-sex-race cohorts within a single group. People who have experienced certain events at particular times in their lives do not later behave in the same way as people who have had other experiences. To have entered the labor force at the onset of a depression or to have reached the age of conscription at the height of the Vietnam conflict could affect future behavior as profoundly as viral diseases at particular stages of embryonic development. We have not as yet spelled out the way in which the time and place of birth or residence in different stages of the life cycle affect behavior over the course of a lifetime, and we have doubtless confused cohort effects with those attributed to age alone or to race, education, or income. While complex, it is expected that both individual (actor) social context and cohort effects are measurable, and consequently, their relevance to simulation can be determined.

As noted, Birch is in search of a generalized model of actor behavior that, when established, will make recalibration of his model unnecessary. He thinks this is possible—others do not. Some people feel that neighborhood, central place, and generation effects are such that some recalibration in the general model will be required as the model is moved from place to place or time period to time period. However, even though Birch is in search of a general model, the current model is able to take place and time effects into account. This is because it allows for adjustment for different localities.

PROBABILITIES AND CONSTRAINTS

The Birch model operates in terms of probabilities and constraints. This was perceived as a significant advance. Rather than taking the position that a rule of behavior implies a uniform mode of behavior, he assumes that in any situation a number of behaviors are possible and his rules of behavior are statements about the probability that a set of behaviors will occur. For example, probabilities determined nationally might indicate that out of a given number of residents belonging to a class determined on the basis of several criteria, a certain number would move from one dwelling unit to another. But constraints are imposed by local situations. Once a preliminary decision has been made to move, there are considerations of the types of neighborhoods within a certain distance, and considerations of cost and time of commuting to work. For example, it was noted that whites are reluctant to move into a black neighborhood, and blacks are almost as unlikely to move into a predominantly white neighborhood. White employed males tend to remain within the same sector of the city as they move from one neighborhood to another, and they try to achieve a commuting time to work of not more than 35 minutes. With such behavior operationally described in terms of probability distributions, it is possible to estimate where people are likely to move. Thus, movement is predictable with respect to direction and is narrowly constrained by distance from the original residence and by distance from work.

WORKPLACE AND HOMEPLACE

While the Birch model avoids the single-minded concentration on economic matters that vitiates most of the models that have been developed by economists, it does not minimize the importance of land use and job location. The Birch model has the advantage of simultaneously taking into account the existing dwelling units in neighborhoods within the usual distance over which people move, the vacancy rate for such dwellings (including the fact that an outmigrant leaves behind an empty dwelling unit and occupies another), the erection of new houses or apartments, and the job locations for persons of a particular group. These are not easy matters to deal with, and the apparent success of the Birch procedure in widely spaced and very different cities speaks for the ingenuity of the MIT-Harvard team, as well as for the wide applicability of the procedure.

FUTURE APPLICATIONS

The potentialities of the Birch simulation model were clearly recognized by conference participants. However, since it is functioning successfully in only a few widely varying places for a comparatively short time period, concern about its reliability and validity are warranted. Additional testing should be encouraged and supported. The 1980 Census will provide an opportunity for assessing reliability and for adjusting the model. Favorable results would lead to the conclusion that the Birch model should be more widely used—that it should be experimented with at the state level with counties as well as smaller areas as the units of analysis.

Encouraging the use of the Birch model is the fact that the procedures are not as expensive as they seem at first glance. There is the cost of installation and of training personnel. Beyond that, however, ongoing operations tend to be relatively cheap and could more than pay for themselves in making data of many sorts easily available for policy-making purposes. Undoubtedly, the cost of the kind of ignorance under which most state administrators labor is greater than the cost of an adequate data system. Providing impetus to such installations is the refusal of the Congress to fund a mid-decade census and the undoubted furor that will follow the 1980 Census publications as states, cities, municipalities, and counties contest the census results in the courts.

A CAUTION BASED ON WORKSHOP MATERIALS

A caution about the use of the Birch model is necessary. Since only the general outline of the Birch simulation procedures was presented at the workshop, it was not possible to evaluate the total model and its numerous subcomponents. There was consensus that the potentialities of the model are such that scholars must invest the time to understand both the general nature of the model and its specific operational procedures. It is only under such conditions that an adequate assessment can be done. Birch, in fact, cautions that his simulation models currently are to be viewed as learning tools. This means that they are still in the developmental stage requiring recalibration as they are moved from city to city. Because in the cities where they have been established, the Birch procedures provide accurate detailed estimates of population characteristics, there should be some way to combine the in-depth Birch-type simulation procedure with the area estimation procedures and thereby provide low-cost small area estimates.

Part Six

Using Area Cohort Procedures

13

A Social Area Analysis Approach

Harold F. Goldsmith,
David J. Jackson,
and J. Philip Shambaugh

INTRODUCTION

Social area analysis explores the relevance of urban residential structure for social processes. Social areas are subareas of a city with similar population and housing characteristics. The distribution of social areas within cities and the distribution of populations across social areas is considered to be the residential structure of a metropolitan area. Residential structure, of course, is not static, but expresses and reflects the growth or decay of metropolitan areas (Beshers, 1962; Timms, 1971).

In this chapter, we hypothesize that similar types of social areas experience similar rates of change, and consequently, that this information allows one to make reasonable estimates of the demographic characteristics of small areas. Admittedly, this is not a refined hypothesis; however, it is a starting point for the examination of data. While national surveys conducted at regular intervals provide useful trend information on characteristics such as household income at the national and regional level, similar data for small or subcounty areas are not available. However, it might be feasible to use national survey data along with a social area typology of census tracts to develop an estimation procedure that would provide reliable trend data for some types of social areas. This would require that a survey of households contain codes for residential tracts and that tracts be classified into social areas. It would then be possible to estimate trends by type of social area. Depending on the sample size and distribution of types of tracts, trends for types of social areas by other characteristics, such as region or central city, could also be estimated. These trend estimates could then be used in the estimation of census tract characteristics. This is an intriguing possibility, however, evidence is lacking to warrant the actual development of a social area type estimation procedure. This chapter explores the potential of a social area typology approach to small area estimation.

SOCIAL AREA ANALYSIS

Social area analysis is predicated on the long-recognized fact that the distribution of urban populations is not random. Furthermore, there is clear evidence that the distribution of urban populations can be described in terms of a small number of social indicators. These indicators locate populations with common social and economic characteristics. Moreover, such populations not only tend to have similar behaviors and attitudes, but behaviors and attitudes that are different for areas with different social and economic characteristics (see Berry and Kasarda, 1977).

Based on an examination of recent literature, we believe that people in the United States generally select residences on the basis of their ability to procure goods and services, their status role obligations, and their desired residential lifestyles. Thus, the most crucial dimensions to be reflected in small area indicators are social rank (and its components: economic class, social class, and educational status), family status, family lifecycle, residential lifestyle (and its components: area house type and area housing conditions), and community stability (Goldsmith and Unger, 1970; Redick et al., 1971; Rosen et al., 1979).

Moreover, the major racial and ethnic populations should be considered separately (Goldsmith, 1972). We also speculate that the order in which the dimensions are presented above may indicate their relative importance for understanding behavior associated with residence (Goldsmith et al., 1978). A typology of social areas can be achieved by simply classifying census tracts by seven key social area dimensions categorized into high, medium, and low, or other significant strata. (For a detailed presentation of the typological approach to social area analysis see Goldsmith et al., 1975.)

PROCEDURES AND DATA

If the hypothesis that similar social areas change in a similar manner is reasonable, it should be possible to use known rates of change of demographic characteristics to estimate the demographic characteristics of social areas for which rates of change are unknown. Such estimates should be better than estimates in which social areas are not controlled. Rate data for the Baltimore SMSA are used to explore this issue. Two procedures for estimating 1970 tract variables for tracts in Montgomery and Prince George's counties, Maryland, are compared. The first procedure uses average 1960-1970 social area specific rates of change; the second, 1960-1970 SMSA average rates of change. In both cases, the rates are calculated for tracts in the Baltimore SMSA.

The analysis of 1960-1970 rates of change for Baltimore area tracts by type of social area proceeded in four stages: (a) the definition of tract level areas that are common in the 1960 and 1970 censuses; (b) the social area classification of the 1960 tracts; (c) the description of the rates of change for fifteen selected variables by type of 1960 social area in the Baltimore SMSA; and (d) the consequences of the use of social area specific change rates to estimate demographic variables.

COMPARABLE GEOGRAPHIC AREAS

The procedures by which geographically comparable areas were defined for 1960 and 1970 census tracts in the 1960 Baltimore SMSA (Baltimore City, Baltimore, Anne Arundel, Carroll, and Howard counties) and the Maryland portion of the 1960 Washington SMSA (Montgomery and Prince George's counties) are presented in Appendix 14.1. Basically, sets of 1970 tracts were aggregated to 1960 tracts with common boundaries. In the following discussion, we will use the convenient label "tracts," to refer to this set of geographically comparable areas.

SOCIAL AREA CLASSIFICATION

The 1960 census tracts (451) in the Maryland area were classified into 27 social area types based upon the following dimensions:

(1) *Ethnicity:* percentage of household population that is black
(2) *Economic status (white population):* median income of white families
(3) *Educational status (white population):* median years of school completed by white persons 25 and over
(4) *Family status (white population):* A composite measure in which tracts are classified along a continuum from white husband-wife family areas to white nonfamily areas (see Goldsmith et al., 1975 for a detailed description of coding procedures)
(5) *Family life-cycle (white population):* Classification of census tracts by the family life cycle stage of the white population (see Goldsmith et al., 1975 for a detailed description of coding procedures)
(6) *House type(nonblack):* percentage of nonblack dwelling units that are single detached

Data from the Mental Health Demographic Profile System (MHDPS) are utilized in this study (Goldsmith et al., 1975).

Because of the small number of census tracts, several modifications of the standard typological procedures had to be made. The dimensions of overcrowding and social status were dropped. Social status, usually indexed by an occupational indicator such as percentage of males in low status occupations, was not used because occupational and educational status tend to be correlated. Overcrowding was dropped because we felt its contribution was largely accounted for by the remaining variables. Even for the dimensions that were used (ethnicity [percentage black], white economic status, white educational status, white family status, white family life-cycle, and non-black house type) many of the standard categories had to be combined to achieve sufficient cases for analysis. The demographic characteristics of the 27 social area types derived for the 1960 census tracts are presented in Table 13.1, along with the distribution of census tracts of the Baltimore and Washington, D.C. SMSAs by type of social area. Operational procedures are summarized in Appendix 13.2. Examination of Table 13.1 reveals that only 5 types (2, 3, 8, 11, and 21) have enough tracts in the Baltimore SMSA and Montgomery and Prince George's counties to make tract cohort estimation procedures feasible.

ANALYSIS OF RATES OF CHANGE BY SOCIAL AREA

Any variables existing in both 1960 and 1970 could be used as test variables. We chose to look at the following MHDPS variables:

(1) total population (MHDPS Table 5, Item 1)
(2) population black (MHDPS Table 5, Item 6)
(3) household population under 18 (numerator of MHDPS Table 5, Item 18)
(4) household population 18 to 64 (denominator of MHDPS Table 5, Item 18)
(5) household population 65 and over (numerator of MHDPS Table 5, Item 18)

TABLE 13.1   Social Area Analysis Typology Code Summary: Maryland Census Tracts in the Baltimore and Washington, D.C. SMSA

| | | | | SOCIAL AREA DIMENSIONS | | | Frequency |
Type Code	Percent Black	Economic Status	Educational Status	Family Status	Family Life Cycle	Housing Type	Baltimore SMSA (Washington, D. C. SMSA)
TOTAL	—	—	—	—	—	—	320
1	≤30	—	—	Husband-wife or Family Area (predominantly husband-wife)	Childbearing	—	3 (5)
2	≤30	Moderate or High	Moderate or High	Husband-wife	Childbearing to Early Childrearing	Single Dwelling Units	47 (10)
3	≤30	Moderate or High	Moderate or High	Husband-wife	Childbearing to Early Childrearing	Not Single Dwelling Units	15 (20)
4	≤30	Low	Moderate or High	Husband-wife or Family Area (predominantly husband-wife)	Childbearing to Early Childrearing	—	6 (1)
5	≤30	Low	Low	Husband-wife or Family Area (predominantly husband-wife)	Childbearing to Early Childrearing	Single Dwelling Units	13 (0)
6	≤30	—	—	—	Childbearing to Early Childrearing	—	22 (0)
7	≤30	Moderate or High	Moderate or High	Husband-wife	Early Childrearing	Not Single Dwelling Units	2 (6)

174

8	≤30	Moderate or High	Moderate or High	Husband-wife	Early Childrearing	Single Dwelling Units	26 (34)
9	≤30	Low	Moderate or High	Husband-wife or Family Area (predominantly husband-wife) and other Family Areas	Early Childrearing	—	1 (3)
10	≤30	Low	Low	Husband-wife or Family Area (predominantly husband-wife)	Early Childrearing	Single Dwelling Units	4 (0)
11	≤30	Moderate or High	Moderate or High	Husband-wife	Middle Childrearing	Single Dwelling Units	17 (13)
12	≤30	Moderate or High	Moderate or High	Husband-wife or Family Area (predominantly husband-wife)	Middle Childrearing	Not Single Dwelling Units	1 (3)
13	≤30	Low	Low	Husband-wife or Family Area (predominantly husband-wife)	Middle Childrearing	Single Dwelling Units	5 (0)
14	≤20	—	—	—	Middle Childrearing	—	5 (0)
15	≤30	Moderate or High	Moderate or High	Husband-wife or Family Area (predominantly husband-wife)	Late Childrearing and Childlaunching	Single Dwelling Units	1 (0)
16	≤30	Low	Moderate or High	Husband-wife or Family Area (predominantly husband-wife)	Late Childrearing and Childlaunching	Not Single Dwelling Units	2 (2)
17	≤30	—	—	—	Late Childrearing and Childlaunching	—	3 (1)
18	≤30	Moderate or High	Moderate or High	Husband-wife or Family Area (predominantly husband-wife)	Post Childlaunching	Single Dwelling Units	5 (0)

(continued)

TABLE 13.1 Continued

			SOCIAL AREA DIMENSIONS				Frequency Baltimore SMSA (Washington, D. C. SMSA)
Type Code	Percent Black	Economic Status	Educational Status	Family Status	Family Life Cycle	Housing Type	
19	≤30	Moderate or High	Moderate or High	Husband-wife or Family Area (predominantly husband-wife)	Post Childlaunching	Not Single Dwelling Units	2 (0)
20	≤30	Low	Moderate or High	Not Nonfamily Areas	Post Childlaunching	—	4 (0)
21	≤30	Moderate or High	Low	Not Nonfamily Areas	Post Childlaunching	—	42 (20)
22	≤30	Low	Low	Husband-wife or Family Area (predominantly husband-wife)	Post Childlaunching	—	34 (0)
23	≤30	—	—	—	Post Childlaunching	—	1 (0)
24	≤30	Moderate or High	Moderate or High	Nonfamily	Post Childlaunching	Not Single Dwelling Units	1 (0)
25	≤30	Low	Moderate or High	Nonfamily	—	Not Single Dwelling Units	2 (1)
26	30-70	—	—	—	—	—	25 (0)
27	≥70	—	—	—	—	—	31 (0)

(6) percentage households husband-wife (MHDPS Table 5, Item 15)
(7) percentage households husband-wife: white (MHDPS Table 6, Item 52)
(8) median income of families and unrelated individuals (MHDPS Table 5, Item 7)
(9) median income of families: white (MHDPS Table 6, Item 11)
(10) median educational level: persons 25 and over (MHDPS Table 5, Item 11)
(11) median educational level: persons 25 and over: white (MHDPS Table 6, Item 34)
(12) youth dependency ratio (MHDPS Table 5, Item 17)
(13) aged dependency ratio (MHDPS Table 5, Item 18)
(14) percentage of dwelling units: single detached (MHDPS Table 5, Item 19)
(15) percentage of population migrants (MHDPS Table 6, Item 94)

In Table 13.2, we present the means and standard deviations of the 1960-1970 change rates of the selected demographic characteristics for five types of social areas in the Baltimore SMSA that were also present in sufficient number in Montgomery and Prince George's counties. An examination of this table reveals that there is considerable variation in change rates among the five types. For example, the 1960-1970 rate of change for total population goes from 16.4 for Type 21 to 76.2 for Type 2.

SMALL AREA ESTIMATION

As noted, the 1970 values of the 15 variables for selected tracts in Montgomery and Prince George's counties were estimated by using 1960-1970 rates of change derived from tracts in the 1960 Baltimore SMSA. Two types of rates were employed: (1) social area type specific mean rates; and (2) the mean rate of change for *all tracts* in the 1960 Baltimore SMSA.

In evaluating the results of our analysis, two questions were considered. They are: (1) Are the estimates based on census tracts classified by social areas significàntly better than those

TABLE 13.2 Mean and Standard Deviation of 1960 to 1970 Percent Rates of Change for Five Social Areas in Baltimore SMSA

Variable	Social Area Type				
	2	3	8	11	21
Total Population	76.17 * (97.04)**	19.40 (41.86)	60.07 (176.53)	28.56 (28.39)	16.39 (26.60)
Population Black	2781.53 (16647.99)	7707.03 (22497.37)	515.41 (1355.67)	207.32 (663.82)	14665.93 (49207.83)
Population Under 18	111.70 (130.90)	35.60 (81.70)	91.50 (276.60)	55.80 (42.00)	66.70 (66.70)
Population 18-64	82.50 (95.40)	18.20 (44.30)	66.10 (167.90)	32.30 (27.90)	9.30 (28.60)
Population 65 and Over	79.40 (63.80)	55.40 (44.10)	71.00 (47.40)	52.60 (47.90)	24.90 (61.50)
Median Income: Families and Unrelated Individuals	77.88 (30.24)	43.93 (11.58)	66.04 (16.39)	63.32 (22.73)	45.49 (18.78)
Median Income: White Families	77.72 (19.04)	54.77 (11.03)	68.15 (14.77)	67.16 (17.76)	52.91 (20.68)

Median Education: Persons ≥25	10.87 (7.65)	2.78 (4.02)	5.56 (6.85)	11.06 (9.02)	5.08 (5.42)
Median Education: White Persons ≥25	9.56 (6.48)	2.28 (4.00)	5.10 (6.43)	10.16 (8.39)	3.62 (5.74)
Percentage Households Husband-Wife Families	-7.25 (6.14)	-14.52 (5.61)	-7.32 (4.04)	-7.37 (7.08)	-12.88 (7.30)
Percentage White Household Husband-Wife Families	-10.75 (6.73)	-16.99 (8.50)	-9.60 (5.27)	-9.56 (7.63)	-18.61 (10.50)
Youth Dependency Ratio	14.32 (15.22)	15.40 (13.58)	4.93 (16.28)	17.12 (14.59)	53.68 (51.13)
Aged Dependency Ratio	9.35 (38.35)	41.36 (46.29)	24.02 (35.87)	16.97 (32.73)	16.10 (48.64)
Percentage Housing Units Single Detached	-29.79 (28.11)	-56.35 (31.82)	-32.62 (31.88)	-19.84 (24.04)	-46.77 (29.96)
Percentage Population Migrants	-14.57 (45.51)	-16.57 (37.15)	-34.59 (34.84)	3.11 (70.27)	24.39 (59.96)
Number of Tracts	47	15	26	17	42

* Mean rate of change 1960 to 1970

** Standard deviation of rates of change 1960 to 1970

based on all tracts; and (2) are the errors in the estimates based on the classification of census tracts by social area types of a scale that would make them acceptable for use in planning?

The statistics utilized, average absolute percentage errors, to answer the above questions are presented below:

$$\sum_{j=1}^{J} \sum_{i=1}^{n_j} \left[\frac{\mid X_{70\,ij} - X_{60ij}\,(1-r_j)\mid}{NX_{70\,ij}} \right] 100 \quad [1]$$

In this equation r_j is the mean rate of change of a given variable for the n_j tracts within the jth type of social area in the Baltimore SMSA and X_{70ij} and X_{60ij} are the values of the given variables for 1970 and 1960, respectively.

$$\sum_{j=1}^{J} \sum_{i=1}^{n_j} \left[\frac{\mid X_{70ij} - X_{60ij}\,(1+r)\mid}{NX_{70\,ij}} \right] 100 \quad [2]$$

In this case r is the mean rate of change for all tracts in the Baltimore SMSA.

Values of the statistics for each variable are presented in columns 1 and 7 of Table 13.3. Examination of these two columns reveals that for all variables except Total Population and Population Under 18 (rows 1 and 3) some reduction in the error level was accomplished by classifying census tracts into social area types. However, some of the changes are small. To evaluate the significance of the changes, the differences (i.e., relative improvement) between the error based on all tracts and the error based on classification by social area is presented in column 8 of Table 13.3. Examination of this column reveals that extremely large (greater than 30 scale points), and consequently very significant reductions occurred for four variables: Black Population, Youth Dependency Ratio, Aged Dependency Ratio, and Percentage Population Migrants. For the remaining eleven variables, the change in percentage error was less than five scale points. If one is willing to allow that an error reduction of four or five scale points is a modest but useful improvement in estimation, then such improvements occur for two of the eleven variables in which error reduction was less than five scale points—Median Education of White Persons 25 and Over, and Percentage White Households that are Husband-Wife Families. Thus, taking both the variables for which significant and modest improvement occurred, useful improvements were achieved by the social area cohort procedures for six of the fifteen variables. Improvements were concentrated among the percentage or ratio variables. Of the five population variables (rows 1-5 of Table 13.3); only one, Population Black, showed a useful improvement as against five of eleven ratio or percentage variables (rows 6-15).

For three sets of variables (Income—rows 6 and 7 of Table 13.3, Education—rows 8 and 9, and Percentage Households Husband-Wife Families—rows 10 and 11), we had data for both total and white populations. For two, Median Education and Percentage Households Husband-Wife Families, the white population, but not the total population had useful reductions in percentage error when social areas were controlled. Most likely this reflects the use of white social area characteristics in the analysis. Unfortunately, neither of the income statistics had a useful decline.

The fact that useful improvements were obtained for nearly half of the ratio or percentage variables does not tell us if the estimates are immediately useful for planning. To ascertain this, one must study columns 1 and 3 of Table 13.3 simultaneously. We will consider an average absolute percentage error as indicating estimates immediately useful for planning if it is less than 10 percent (see column 1) and potentially useful if less than 30 percent. These standards may appear to be lax, but the period of estimation covers a ten-year span. We assume that if similar procedures were used for a shorter period the errors would be considerably smaller. Applying the above standards to column 1

TABLE 13.3 Summary of Errors in Estimation from 1960 to 1970 for All Census Tracts and Census Tracts Classified by Social Areas in Prince George's and Montgomery Counties Using 1960-1970 Rates of Change for Social Areas in the Baltimore SMSA

Row		All Areas Col. 1	Average Percentage Error for Social Area Types[1]					Nonspecific Rates[2] Col. 7	Difference (Col. 7 – Col. 1) Col. 8
			2 Col. 2	3 Col. 3	8 Col. 4	11 Col. 5	21 Col. 6		
1	Total Population	31.1	21.3	54.3	41.7	20.7	18.2[2]	27.8	-3.3
2	Population Black	2271.1	2038.9	1773.6	170.0	1777.0	6645.3	3951.1	168.0
3	Population Under 18	29.4	23.4	44.2	43.2	12.9	15.4	26.9	-2.5
4	Population 18-64	42.5	27.7	68.7	44.7	35.6	45.1	45.6	3.1
5	Population 65 and Over	25.5	28.2	31.8	24.5	16.6	26.9	27.1	1.6
6	Median Income: Families and Unrelated Individuals	13.0	11.5	13.9	12.4	11.0	16.3	14.6	1.6
7	Median Income: White Families	9.0	9.4	12.4	8.7	8.1	8.2	10.0	1.0
8	Median Education: Persons 25 and Over	4.7	3.5	5.2	4.6	8.3	3.6	6.7	2.0

9	Median Education: White Persons 25 and Over	4.3	3.8	4.9	4.0	7.2	3.0	9.2	4.9
10	Percentage Households Husband-Wife Families	7.0	5.8	5.1	6.2	5.6	11.3	8.1	1.1
11	Percentage White Households Husband-Wife Families	6.7	5.3	4.6	6.3	4.6	11.0	11.6	4.9
12	Youth Dependency Ratio	20.6	14.6	17.8	14.3	10.6	45.3	120.7	100.1
13	Aged Dependency Ratio	39.9	35.3	84.0	48.2	15.9	23.7	70.1	30.2
14	Percentage Housing Units Single Detached	39.6	41.7	56.7	38.4	15.9	43.3	42.2	3.2
15	Percentage Population Migrants	34.8	20.2	33.4	35.4	43.9	43.2	106.5	71.7
	Number of Tracts	131	20	10	34	13	20	131	

[1] The error rates for this column is the average of the absolute percentage error in which rates specific to tract type are used, i.e., the average of

$$\left| \frac{x_{70ijk} - x_{60ijk}(1 + r_{jk})}{x_{70ijk}} \right|$$

x_{60ijk} is the 1960 value of the kth variable for the ith tract in the jth type.

r_{jk} is the 1960-1970 average rate of change for the kth variable and the jth type of area in Baltimore's SMSA.

x_{70ijk} is defined in a similar manner.

[2] The error rate for this column is similar to column 1; however, a common rate of change is used, i.e.,

$r_{jk} = r_k$ is the average rate of change between 1960 and 1970 for the kth variable without respect to type of tract.

of Table 13.3, we find that the following nine variables meet
our criteria:

Error 10%-29.9%

- Population Under 18
- Population 65 and Over

- Youth Dependency Ratio

- Median Income Families
  and Unrelated Individuals

Error Less Than 10%

- Median Income: White Families
- Percentage Households Husband-
  Wife Families
- Percentage White Households
  Husband-Wife Families
- Median Education: Persons Over
  25 Years
- Median Education: White Per-
  sons Over 25 Years

Of the nine variables listed above, only the Youth Dependency Ratio, Median Education White Persons 25 and over, and
Percentage White Households Husband-Wife Families have
moderate or high error reductions. Of the remaining variables,
the magnitude of improvement in estimation was less than four
scale points, and accordingly, not considered significant. This
means that for these variables one does almost as well not
controlling the type of social area.

The social area cohort procedures may produce significantly
better results for some social areas than for others. If this is
true, the aggregate results previously discussed would not yield
dramatic improvements in estimation. Table 13.3 shows that
some of the social area types did have small or moderate
percentage errors even when the average absolute error for a
variable was high, or considerable reductions in error when both
average measures are similar (a difference of less than 4 percent
error scale points). Listed below are the social area types by
variables in which the error level is less than thirty and the

difference between the type error level and the average aggregate error level is four or more scale points:

Variable	Type
• Total Population	2, 11, 21
• Population Under 18	11, 21
• Population 18-64	2
• Population 65 and Over	8, 11
• Youth Dependency Ratio	2, 8, 11
• Aged Dependency Ratio	11
• Percentage Households Single Dwelling Units	11
• Percentage Population Migrants	2

Compared to the error rate for all areas, these social area types
have lower error levels for all variables except Population 65
and Over. Clearly, for at least half the variables, social area
types 2 and 11 have both error levels and error reductions
within the limits we consider useful for planning and estimation
improvement.

If the patterns observable in Table 13.3 have an acceptable
degree of reliability, then one may conclude that some social
areas such as social area types 2 or 11 have error levels for many
demographic variables that are consistently moderate or low
and significantly below the error levels based on tracts not
classified by social areas.

CONCLUSION

In this chapter, we have demonstrated that the use of social
areas in estimating the demographic characteristics of census
tracts does provide data for some areas that are useful for
planning. We calculated the rates of 1960-1970 change for a set
of demographic variables using the census tracts of the Baltimore SMSA *in toto* or classified by social areas. Two sets of

rates were then used to estimate the demographic characteristics in Montgomery and Prince George's Counties. In a number of cases, the use of social areas improved the estimates so much that the procedure warrants systematic investigation to establish reliability and to identify and control sources of error.

It must be remembered that even though this demonstration provided interesting results, it was not intended as a final procedure. Rather, we feel that an appropriately modified procedure would provide good estimates for at least five years after a census. The ten-year period was selected for convenience. A similar procedure should be developed using data from large surveys such as the Current Population Surveys. Respondents could be geocoded to tract and classified by type of social area in which they resided.

We suggest that one begin by identifying the kinds of factors that affect population change in small areas. For example, at any given time a type of social area can change in a limited number of ways. If these patterns can be identified and their probabilities established, a series of short-term estimates (under five years) can be made. The kinds of factors that one expects are linked to residential change in small areas are accessibility to employment, good schools, shopping facilities, availability of land for new construction, condition of housing, ethnic-race composition, as well as the economic and social structure of central places. As a prelude to such an analysis we now plan to explore the kinds of residential changes that have taken place within small residential areas between 1960-1970.

In conclusion, it is our feeling, after having carried out the analysis in this chapter, that the use of social areas can considerably improve the estimation of small area demographic characteristics. It is a procedure that has received little attention. We recommend that it be used in additional demonstrations, particularly ones in which the time period for the estimation is reduced.

REFERENCES

BERRY, B.J.L. and J. D. KASARDA (1977) Contemporary Urban Ecology. New York: Macmillan.

BESHERS, J. W. (1962) Urban Social Structure. Glencoe, IL: Free Press.

GOLDSMITH, H. F. (1972) "Small area demographic profiles," pp. 71-99 in A. L. Ferriss (ed.) Research and the 1970 Census. Oak Ridge, TN: Southern Regional Demographic Group.

——— D. J. JACKSON, B. M. ROSEN, and H. BABIGIAN (1978) "Utilization of mental health services." Presented at the Second National Conference on Need to understanding the relationships between social rank and the utilization of mental health services." Presented at the Second National Conference on Needs Assessment in Health and Human Services, Louisville, Kentucky.

GOLDSMITH, H. F. and E. L. UNGER (1970) "Differentiation of urban subareas: a re-examination of social area dimensions." Laboratory Paper No. 35. Adelphi, MD. Mental Health Study Center, National Institute of Mental Health, November.

——— B. M. ROSEN, J. P. SHAMBAUGH, and C. D. WINDLE (1975) "A typological approach to doing social area analysis." Mental Health Statistics Series C, No. 10, National Institute of Mental Health.

REDICK, R. W., H. F. GOLDSMITH, and E. L. UNGER (1971) "1970 census data used to indicate areas with different potentials for mental health related problems." Methodological Reports, Series C, No. 3, National Institute of Mental Health. Rockville, MD: Health Service and Mental Health Administration.

ROSEN, B. M., H. F. GOLDSMITH, and R. W. REDICK (1979) "Demographic and social indicators from the U.S. Census of Population and Housing: uses for mental health planning in small areas." *World Health Statistics. Quarterly Report 32, 1: 11-102.*

TIMMS, D.W.G. (1971) The Urban Mosaic. Cambridge: Cambridge Univ. Press.

APPENDIX 13.1: TRACT COMPARABILITY

The keystone to building a data file for this estimation model is geographic comparability between two points in time. Ideally, each 1960 tract would have had no boundary changes between 1960-1970, but would have been split into pieces as necessary to accommodate growth in the area during the decade. Unfortunately, this was not the case. The Bureau of the Census did print tract comparability lists for 1960 and 1970 tracts,

TABLE 13.A1 Number of Tract Records by County, Maryland

	1960	1970	Merged File
Anne Arundel	40	72	40
Baltimore	126	190	121
Baltimore City	168	206	142
Carroll	11	21	11
Howard	6	18	6
Montgomery	60	122	57
Prince George's	74	143	74
TOTAL	485	772	451

including a "part" designation when boundaries did not coincide. To define common geographic areas, all of "part" designations must be added together, thus reducing the number of individual areas and muddying the small area statistics by aggregation to larger units. The problem is that these published lists provide exact geographic area correspondence whether or not any population was affected. For example, a 1960 tract may have included a cemetery; in 1970 that tract was split and at the same time redrawn to exclude the cemetery. This would force the aggregation of two or more *1960* tracts to match to the *1970* tracts of the same geography. Many tracts were redrawn as a consequence of the beltways circling the cities of Baltimore and Washington, D.C. The new boundary may have affected less than 5 percent of the population, but this cannot be ascertained from the published tract lists. In order to maximize the number of records on the final data set, and minimize the size of these areas, we supplemented the published tract lists with "local area knowledge."

Maps for 1960 and 1970 were obtained that showed block group detail for the cities and population density for some suburbs. By comparing tract boundaries, some approximations were made that considerably increased the number of minimum sized areas. Minimum sized areas were constructed that contained whole tracts for 1960 and for 1970. Only 18 "aggregated" 1960 tracts had to be created in order to achieve comparability, reducing the total from 485 to 451. It should be noted that some of the tracts crossed political boundaries and also had to be aggregated.

The total number of aggregations was 41. We used a rule of thumb limit that 5 percent of the total population of a tract could be affected before we would consider it necessary to create an aggregate area. We violated this rule in the inner city of Baltimore where it would have been necessary to create an area including twelve 1960 tracts. Instead, we made 3 areas out of the 12 tracts with population errors of −6 percent, + 7 percent, and −2 percent (aggregate area numbers 13, 14, 15). This approach to geographic comparability increased the resultant number of merged 1960 and 1970 tracts by about 20 percent with essentially no loss in accuracy. Table 13.A1 shows a summary by county in Maryland of the number of census tracts in both decades and in the merged 1960-1970 file.

APPENDIX 13.2: OPERATIONAL PROCEDURES FOR SOCIAL AREA DIMENSIONS

The indicators used to measure the social area relationships of the populations of the census tracts in this study are presented below. They are social indicators from the Mental Health Demographic Profile System (Goldsmith et al., 1975). With the exception of Percentage Population Black, all reflect characteristics of the white population of census tracts. The classification of areas into high, medium, and low, or other appropriate designations, is based upon *A Typological Approach to Doing Social Area Analysis* (see Goldsmith et al., 1975).

(1) *Economic Status:* Median income of white families for the white population of metropolitan counties.
- High $10,744 or more
- Medium $ 9,303-$10,743
- Low $ 9,302 or less

(2) *Educational Status:* Median years of school completed by white persons 25 years and over.
- High   62.9% or more
- Medium   53.3 to 62.8%
- Low   53.2% or less

(3) *Family Status:* Husband-wife family areas: 70% or more of the households in an area are husband-wife families.

- Family areas—Predominantly husband-wife family areas: 70% of the households in an area are families and 50-59.9% are husband-wife families.
- Other family areas—70% of the households in an area are families and less than 50% are husband-wife.
- Nonfamily areas—70% of the households in an area are nonfamily households.
- Mixed Areas—Areas not classified above.

(4) *Family Life-Cycle* (see Goldsmith et al., 1975: 14-16): Classification of an area according to its family life-cycle classification is based upon the proportion of children in an area in five-year categories and the proportion of the population over 50, 20 to 24, or 25 to 29. In general, the classification of areas is as follows:

- Childbearing—12.5% or more of a population are less than 5 years and 7.5% are less than 5-9 years.
- Early Childrearing—12.5% or more of a population are 5-9 years.
- Middle Childrearing—12.5% or more of a population are 10-14 years.
- Late Childrearing—12.5% or more of a population are 15-19 years.
- Post Childlaunching—25% or more of a population are 50 years and over.
- Prefamily—If persons 20-24 and 25-29 are greater than 12.5% of a population and if persons 0-4 and 5-9 years are less than 7.5% of a population.

(5) *House Type:*

- Single Dwelling Unit Areas—70% or more of dwelling units are single detached.
- Mixed Dwelling Unit Areas—20 to 70% of dwelling units are single detached.
- Apartment House Areas—Less than 20% of the dwelling units are single detached.

14

Evaluation and Synopsis

The Editors

The associations between the demographic data for the 1960
and 1970 Census tracts of metropolitan counties in Maryland
presented by Goldsmith and others (this monograph) clearly
demonstrate that estimation models based on census tract
cohorts classified by social area type (tract-cohort models) may
provide useful estimates of small area population characteristics.
While the model presented was imperfect, it had sufficient merit
to warrant development and further evaluation. The model, as
presented, assumed that tracts of a given social area type change
in a limited number of ways and that some changes are more
likely to occur than others. In some types of tracts, only one
direction of change was highly likely—this is the case in classic
suburban areas—whereas in other types of tracts there were
several equally likely directions of change—such is the case in
many inner city areas. For the former types, estimation is easy
and accurate; for the latter types, difficult and inaccurate.

The fact that potential directions of change can be determined and that estimates using the tract-cohort method can
yield good estimates in some but not all areas has several
consequences. If, as the model suggests, there are a limited
number of directions of change with a probability attached to
each, estimates of population characteristics could be based on
each of the most likely directions of change. The most likely
direction of change could be determined from administrative

records for small areas or from documented changes for the larger area within which a small area is nested; or simply by asking local people to do a quick windshield survey to identify the most likely direction of change within small areas.

No matter how the direction of change is found, local people should be involved in the evaluation of estimates for their communities. This will not only generate more accurate data and promote the use of the data, but will produce a constituency that supports the production of the small area estimates. Also, cohort procedures can be used to sort out the low and high error areas. In low error areas, the estimate can be assumed to be reasonable; however, in high error areas, supplementary information based on administrative records or sample surveys will be needed.

To be effective, the cohort model requires monitoring the direction of demographic change in types of small areas. In this model, this is done by calculating change from one time to another. This procedure identifies the consequences of ongoing social and economic processes, but not the processes themselves. If direct measures of ongoing processes were introduced into the tract-cohort method, considerable error reduction might be achieved. A program linking the simulation model, based on processes, and the tract-cohort model, based on measured change in types of areas, might improve our understanding and use of both models. With respect to the cohort model, Birch's simulation model can serve at least two purposes. First, simulation models for specific cities can assess the probability of different types of change occurring within census tracts. The simulation model in specific cities would act as a detector device for the cohort model. In the absence of other data, this information could be used to identify the most likely directions of demographic change to be used with tract-cohort models. Second, in cities where in-depth simulation models exist, the simulation model provides a check against cohort procedures. Simulation models might be used to recalibrate the cohort model so that it is more effective. If simulation models can be used to link tract-cohort models to the processes of demographic change, then local area simulation can be used to improve national level estimation procedures.

The development of a tract-cohort or similar estimation model requires that federal agencies have a major role in the production and distribution of the requisite data, as well as a major role in the development of models. The linkage of census tract data from the census to tract data from surveys must be done by a federal agency in order to assure privacy. After linkage, specific tract designations could be removed while maintaining the demographic data necessary for the model. Clearly, the development of adequate models will be severely handicapped if the primary role of the federal government is only that of a producer and distributor of data. People who run the census often see their role as simply one of generating information. The kind of data collected and distributed by federal agencies implies a theory of behavior. Consequently, those involved in the production of data should also be involved in the research that identifies the data required for special purposes, including estimation models. While greater governmental support for small area estimates is needed, the federal government cannot be expected to do all the work. Local jurisdictions, states, and universities must be encouraged to join in the tasks of developing small area estimation models. Competing perspectives developed by different groups are more likely to result in useful developments. The general consensus is that greater government support is required, particularly for estimation procedures such as the IRS administrative records procedure or the cohort model which requires government involvement. The wise use of IRS-based estimates by government and businesses illustrates the importance and the low cost of small area data when produced for the nation. Given the necessary role of the federal government, expansion of its role beyond the production of estimates should be encouraged. This encouragement should not, however, reduce the involvement of others in the research and development process.

Since the government restricts access to the largest and most important sets of data needed for small area estimation, we need to find ways to make needed data available while protecting the privacy of the records. We are at the point where major innovations in the distribution of data can take place. At the conference, David Birch suggested the following:

> There is absolutely no reason other than cultural and bureaucratic orientations why the Census Bureau cannot make all of its basic records available to anyone who wants to use them. It is now possible in a time-sharing environment for an individual to select any three or four cross tabulations and portray them in graphic form. You could produce any cross tabulation for any set of census variables for any areas or time period you want. All the software is now available. Furthermore, with two or three people, I'm absolutely persuaded I could set up such a system. Howard Brunsman and I built the original software to do it in the late 1960s and early 1970s. It has all the suppression codes needed to protect privacy. It's relatively simple to operate. The tapes would remain secure at the Bureau of Census, but could be accessed by dialing through existing computer networks. Moreover, by going to a modern, randomly addressed information system, data would be available rapidly at low cost—perhaps three or four dollars for any sort of table.
>
> It should be recognized that the costs of building an interactive system are small. It could be done at a very low cost with a minimum of two or three people. There are no software development costs of any magnitude. It's purely a question of attitude at this point, nothing else.

Part Seven

**The Future of Small Area
Population Estimation**

15

Trends and Prospects

Everett S. Lee,
with Harold F. Goldsmith,
Michael Greenberg,
and Donald B. Pittenger

In conclusion, we shall attempt to put the previous chapters into historical context, check the methods presented or available against relevant criteria, and speculate on the future of small area estimation. We begin by noting that the United States, once the pace setter for other nations in demographic and social accounting, has become statistically a backward nation. It is for this reason that the estimation of populations and their characteristics is more important for the United States than for most other advanced countries.

POPULATION ACCOUNTING IN THE UNITED STATES AND OTHER COUNTRIES

Though the United States was the first country to develop a continuing system of population accounting, it has lagged behind many of the advanced countries in the collection of data on population and housing. The most important information to be collected by any nation is the number, characteristics, distribution, and living conditions of its people. For maximum usefulness these data must be accurate and timely. One would suppose that any one of the more developed countries would set up a system that would provide the requisite data at frequent intervals and make certain they were valid. Indeed most of the developed countries do just that and, except for a few of the poorest or most isolated, the less developed countries, in the interest of development, are setting up censuses or population registers. Of course, we too take a census, but it is taken once in ten years and most of the questions are addressed to a sample of the population. From that sample, some of the most important characteristics of the population are estimated. Thus, the process of estimation begins with the census itself, and involves the imputing of missing items or even "missing persons," and the inflation of the sample to represent total population. For small areas some items are deleted for reasons of sampling variability as well as privacy. Utilizing primarily censuses and periodic sample surveys, the Bureau has amassed useful and relatively accurate data. However, despite the enviable record of the Bureau of the Census, it cannot hope to achieve the levels of completeness and accuracy that are commonly obtained by most of the advanced countries, especially those with small, homogeneous populations. Americans do not welcome the small intrusion into their privacy that the census entails, though it comes but once in ten years, and some groups are actively hostile to it. By contrast, the Dutch think it necessary to maintain in a central register current data on every inhabitant, and the Japanese are so impressed with the usefulness of carefully assembled data that they annually celebrate a holiday known as Statistics Day.

Population registers, as they are found in Sweden, Denmark, the Netherlands, West Germany, Israel, and a number of other countries, include items on each individual along with data on parents, spouse, and children. People are entered in the register at birth with date of birth, sex, and parentage noted. Additional items are entered later—for example, religion, marriage, divorce, education, and occupation. A person migrating from one community to another takes out a migration certificate, one copy of which is sent to the community of destination and another accompanies the migrant. At the destination, the migrant reports to the proper office, which notifies the community of origin that he has arrived. The migrant is then entered on the register at the new community and removed from the register of origin. Thus, from birth to death, a frequently, updated and detailed record is maintained for each person.

In these countries, it is a simple matter to determine the population of each small area at any time. Nevertheless, several countries with population registers also take censuses. These are used to check on the population register and to gather data not obtainable from the register. In keeping with the desire for timely data, these countries usually take censuses at much shorter intervals than we do. Five years is a common intercensal period.

Population registers and frequent censuses indicate the lengths to which other countries are willing to go to avoid the uncertainties we tolerate in regard to population. Of course, we too have long been aware of the need for more frequent information about our people. President Grant, a statesman seldom applauded for his acuity, noted in his Fourth Annual Message to the Congress that "The interval at present established between the Federal census is so long that the information obtained at the decennial period as to the material condition, wants and resources of the nation is of little practical value after the expiration of the first half of that period" (Richardson, 1969). Indeed, one of the few distinctions of the Grant administration was that it was the first to recommend a five-year interval between censuses. Grant was aware, of course, of the political implications, and suggested that the middecade census be "divested of all political character and no reapportionment of Congressional representation be made under it" (Richardson, 1969).

In contrast to the ten-year intervals that separate censuses of population and housing are the four-year intervals between agricultural censuses and the five-year intervals between censuses of business. However, the Constitution requires a reapportionment of the House of Representatives after each

census, and the extension of the "one man—one vote" requirement to states and cities or even counties has greatly increased
the political impact of the census by threatening party control
at the local level. To reapportion the House of Representatives
and to make the now required changes in state and other
political entities is a formidable task, one that few would want
to undertake frequently.

For these and other reasons, mostly economic, the mid-
decade census, which was scheduled to begin in 1985, will not
be conducted. At best there will be a sample survey larger than
the usual Current Population Survey, but far too small to
provide data for small areas. However, it will provide control
totals for larger areas against which included small areas can be
checked. It can also be used to improve estimates of characteristics that are difficult to assess in small areas. More and
more, we are forced to the realization that the proper allocation
of health and other resources depends upon the distribution of
different kinds of people, and when census and register data are
not available we are forced to make estimates. Larger and better
surveys of population and housing, as envisioned at middecade,
will not obviate the need for data for small areas. Thus, instead
of reducing the demand for estimates for small areas, the
reliable information obtained for larger areas from such surveys
will stimulate the demand for small area estimates.

THE LONG HISTORY OF POPULATION ESTIMATION
IN THE UNITED STATES

The practice of estimating population has an old and honored
history in the United States. It began with the estimation of
population for the states, spread to large cities, was eventually
undertaken for counties, and now is done for those thousands
of places that are incorporated or otherwise can claim federal or
state funds. Often, there have been protests against the practice,
yet at each level of aggregation, estimates have proven useful

and feasible, taking into account, of course, the absolute and proportional errors that can be tolerated.

When the founding fathers drew up the Constitution of the United States, they realized that regular censuses (population registers were not considered, though the church registers that were their prototypes were already in existence in Scandanavian countries) were necessary for democracy, for how else could proportional representation be maintained. But in order to set up the House of Representatives it was necessary to estimate the population of the states separately for the free and the slaves—the latter being counted as three-fifths of a person for the purpose of representation and the imposition of direct taxes. These estimates were made quite informally by delegates at the convention, and were used to apportion the 65 members of the first House of Representatives. Made in 1787, they can be compared with the counts made three years later at the first census. Even without making an allowance for differential growth of the states over the intervening three years, the estimates look very good. Indeed, the number of Representatives accorded any one state would not have changed by more than one; Virginia or North Carolina might have gained a Representative and Georgia might have lost one (Bureau of the Census, 1976).

Thus, almost 200 years ago the populations of the United States could be estimated well enough for the purpose of establishing representation in the Congress. Undoubtedly we could still do as well, if we accepted the risk that minor over- or underestimation for a particular state could result in the gain or loss of one Representative. Such a result can depend upon a very small number when the necessary adjustments are made to avoid giving a state a fraction of a representative. Indeed, it is not improbable that estimates for the states would result in no more misallocation of Representatives than does a census. This illustrates another and a major use of population estimates. They are the basis for challenging or correcting a census count.

It is an old story for cities to estimate their populations and challenge decennial census counts. Sometimes the challenges were based on nothing more than casual or biased observations, but on occasion they were carefully constructed. As early as 1890, in the *Special Reports of the 1900 Census,* the Bureau addressed itself to the reliability of existing methods of estimating population. Maintaining that "the results of the Federal census, giving the population of the several states and territories, are accepted without challenge both by the Congress and by the country," the Bureau nevertheless noted that "the accuracy of the figures for the population of a city is sometimes disputed or denied" (Bureau of the Census, 1906).

Admitting that such challenges were often made in good faith, the Bureau set out to examine the data upon which estimates were based and the methodology by which they were prepared. The following ways of estimating total population were listed:

(1) Assume the same annual rate of growth as occurred between the two previous censuses.
(2) Apply some ratio to the number of voters in an election.
(3) Apply some ratio to the number of children in school or counted in school censuses.
(4) Apply some ratio to the number of persons listed in city or other directories.

For a sample of 78 cities the Bureau experimented with each of these methods and found them all wanting. Noting that in more than half of the cities the rate of growth for 1890-1900 differed by 18 percent or more from that for the previous intercensal period, the Bureau dismissed simple extrapolation. Votes cast in an election were found to be highly variable from one city to another, and within cities from time to time. Furthermore, the increase in the number of voters did not run parallel with the increase in population. The number of children discovered in school censuses were seldom taken with sufficient accuracy to be good bases for population estimates.

City directories were dismissed as always resulting in overestimates. Quoting James A. Garfield, who in turn was quoting

Samuel Johnson, the Bureau said: "To count is a modern practice; the ancient method was to guess and where numbers are guessed they are always magnified" (Bureau of the Census, 1906). The Bureau preferred that cities not make estimates, but if they must it suggested arithmetic extrapolation. For that practice the rationale was that it generally gave the best results, at least in the short run, for the cities studied. Interestingly, this technique tends to underestimate where rates of growth are sustained or increased.

SCIENCE OR ART

It still remains embarrassingly true that a simple, dis-ingeneous method will sometimes yield better estimates than elaborate, presumably sophisticated methods. The modern successor to arithmetic or geometric extrapolation is a multiple regression that typically uses such data as school enrollment, motor vehicle registration, resident births, resident deaths, and sales taxes. Undoubtedly, the results of such regressions now in use will be reviewed after the 1980 Census to see if different factors would have given better results. Such techniques have the advantage of relative simplicity and complete empiricism. Furthermore, the collection of data and calculations can be turned over to clerks.

Unfortunately, estimating populations is something like weather forecasting. Standard sets of data can be used in speci-fied ways, but improved forecasts can be made by people who have long-time knowledge of a particular area and understand the special ways in which local weather varies from standard patterns. In many cases the final step in making the best estimate for a local area is not science but art—the tailoring of mechanically obtained results to fit local conditions and make them consonant with estimates for neighboring or encompassing areas. In this regard much progress has been made in recent years. The cooperative program that the Bureau of the Census has set up with the states and the checking of initial returns from the 1980 Census by local authorities are important steps toward achieving a consistent and improved program for local estimates.

But there are problems in any cooperative arrangement no matter how cheerfully entered into, as any husband and wife will attest. In particular, there is the tendency, noted by Samuel Johnson, to overestimate the population. This springs from the usual definition of growth as good, and a willingness to accept increases rather than decreases. In many cases, the purpose of the estimate is to prove that certain monies should be forthcoming or to set the stage for action that will not be taken if growth is lagging. It is all too easy to resolve matters of doubt in favor of growth. For example, Earle Klay found that county commissioners in Florida were almost universally convinced that their counties were growing at about the same rate as the state when, in fact, they were growing much more slowly (Klay, 1974).

ACCEPTABLE ERROR

Almost as harmful to the progress of science as carelessness in measurement is overemphasis on precision, a striving for accuracy in nonsignificant digits. Just as one may need to measure distance to the nearest kilometer or the nearest centimeter, one must be content with population counts to the nearest million or the nearest hundred, depending upon the purpose for which we use the figures. And, if one is wise, one will copy the engineer who estimates the heaviest traffic to which a bridge will be subjected and then build in an additional factor of safety. On the whole, we are accustomed to living with moderate uncertainty, but when it comes to population there is a tendency to be uncomfortable with the slightest suggestion of error. The census, thanks to the high standards that have been maintained throughout its existence and the emphasis we put on equal representation, is almost sacrosanct and the merest suggestion of error comes as a shock.

In fact, the census is intended to count every soul from the last infant to be born to those still expiring. Estimates, however, are another matter. They cannot be exact and we must admit to a variety of biases. Thus we must face the question of acceptable error. Usually we measure error as a percentage difference from an actual census or some other type of count, either of which may be flawed. As we might expect on purely statistical grounds as well as on the basis of available data, percentage errors tend to increase as the size of the areas for which estimates are made decrease. For the United States we may expect the error to be minor, probably no more than the usual undercount of three percent or so. For states it will vary a great deal but generally in relation to size. For California and New York the percentage error should be small, but for Nevada or Montana it could be large. Similar considerations apply to counties; the larger the county, the less the percentage error. For these areas we have evaluations of estimates, published after censuses, which go back three decades, but for areas below the county level we have had no major evaluations.

If we had evaluations of estimates for small areas, they would undoubtedly show quite large percentage errors. This, of course, is to be expected because of the data on which they are based and because of statistical variation. This we must accept but we should raise the question as to how much error is acceptable and what kinds of errors are most acceptable. For example, when we evaluate population estimates for states and counties we hope to find that the average error is small—the nearer to zero the better. Additionally, we would like to find about the same number of estimates that were high as low but clustered closely around the average error.

An important question is that of percentage versus numerical error. For many small areas, the percentage errors in population estimates will seem large, say 20 percent. But is a 20 percent error crucial for a little populated area? Would it matter very much if the estimated population of Loving County, Texas, were 50 percent higher than the population enumerated in the 1980 Census? That would be an error of something less than 50 people in a quite extensive county. For areas with large populations, the percentage error is usually the most meaningful statistic; a 1 percent error for California represents a large number of people and could cost the state hundreds of thousands of dollars. On the other hand, an error of 10,000 is a negligible matter for the state.

Very little thought has been given to the dispersion of error around the mean. Indeed, we will doubtless find different mean errors and different dispersions of errors around the mean not only for different techniques of estimation, but also for areas of different size, location, or composition when the same method of estimation is used. Therefore, we must continue to ask ourselves not only how widely applicable the technique may be and the magnitude of the error to be expected, but also whether the technique will have a greater or lesser spread of error for different size or type of places.

EVALUATION OF SELECTED METHODS OF ESTIMATION

Donald Pittenger, who has had long experience with population estimates for small areas, has listed several criteria against which the different methods should be assessed. The first is accuracy, the second is cost, the third is the detail obtainable, and last, but by no means least, is privacy. Utilizing these criteria, and comparing the census and various methods of estimation against population registers, which are generally up to date, and permit balance sheets of population to be made at any time, the population registers' accuracy is very good and the cost may be moderate. There is, however, the key question of privacy. With population registers, the state can follow the individual through life, even through generations. The registers are always available for the use of the state, and sometimes they are open to the general public. To Americans the possibility of the invasion of privacy and the misuse of records by the state has precluded population registers in this country, but the continuing and mounting invasion by illegal immigrants may soon force such a system. Indeed, there may be no other way to protect ourselves.

Furthermore, since we are not willing to face the cost and political implications of a quinquennial census, we must consider expansion of the Current Population Survey, regularly conducted by the Bureau of the Census, from which estimates of population and population characteristics are made for the nation, its regions, the combination of metropolitan areas, and sometimes for states. It is not unlikely that the sample size for these surveys will be expanded and that estimates can and will be made regularly for states and agglomerations of equal population. Unfortunately, such surveys will not provide estimates for small areas. Obviously, we shall continue to need and make estimates for small areas. Moreover, as concern for the environment mounts because of differential change in population characteristics or production, the need for timely and accurate information about the number and characteristics of population in small areas will mount.

Consistently it was noted at the conference that there is a place for the simplest, crudest, roughest methods of estimation, arithmetic extrapolations, component methods, and synthetic procedures, especially for the years just after a census. It is entirely reasonable to use such procedures at times because they are cheap and because they are likely to be accurate enough for most purposes. In some instances it may even pay to accept the early recommendation of the Bureau of the Census to avoid estimations if possible.

Among the comparatively simple methods are those presented by Peter Francese. He illustrated two procedures utilized by private profit-making marketing organizations for estimating population characteristics. Based on the assumption that similar areas have similar rates of demographic change, these organizations have developed regression models to estimate intercensal small area population characteristics such as per capita income and household income. They utilize the best survey and local census data available for the estimation data. These models are not expensive because they are generally based on readily available but nonrepresentative samples of small areas—affluent suburban areas are likely to be overrepresented, whereas poor inner-city areas are likely to be underrepresented. Because suburban areas are well represented and do not change in an erratic manner, small area estimates for such areas can be expected to be reasonable. Unfortunately, a similar statement cannot be made for central city neighborhoods. For such areas, the assumption that similar areas undergo similar change is less likely to be valid. For distributions, these organizations assume that change in a characteristic such as the income distribution for large areas (SMSAs or cities) is constant across all small areas nested within them, and that the relative position of a nested area remains constant over time. These are unrealistic assumptions, but as with ratio and percentage estimated from the regression models, their goal is not a precise estimate for a specific small area, but the use estimate for a set of areas for a marketing decision. Since population characteristic is only one element of a number of elements in this decision, a high degree of precision is not required.

The Rive's Survey Method, which is envisioned as involving a survey concomitant with a census, and using a ratio between the two to apply to the results of a similar survey for estimates at a later time, is a straightforward method, simple in conception and difficult in procedure. As propounded, it has the disadvantage of being expensive, but the distinct advantage of providing detailed and accurate estimates of population characteristics. Moreover, it is hard to imagine later users of population estimates taking a survey at the time of a census to be used some years later in an estimation procedure. However, the method could well be recommended to the Bureau of the Census which can sample its own records at any time and survey either the persons or the locations selected whenever it chooses.

In fact, such a procedure recommends itself to any organization, such as the Social Security Administration or the Internal Revenue Service, that wishes to assess change within its own rolls. The procedure should produce reliable estimates. An alternate procedure is to take a survey at the time estimates are desired, match the localities or persons with census or other data at the beginning of a period, and thus assess changes. Of course, we can expect a set of problems peculiar to a "reverse" approach that are different from the "forward" approach proposed by Rives. These need to be explicated, particularly since the "forward" approach applies best to areas with stable housing structures. Identification of such areas would require the development of an effective system that monitors the direction of small area social change. Certainly such a monitoring system, perhaps based on a systematic examination of 1970-1980 change in small areas, should be encouraged.

The Census Bureau's use of IRS records is simply one of many possible uses of administrative records as a part of a component approach to population estimation. The Census Bureau estimates migration from changes in addresses of taxpayers from one year to the next. In the main, the IRS records are the most desirable for this purpose because they cover so large a part of the population and because there are penalties attached to not filing or giving false information. Though the Internal Revenue Service would protest the idea, it is conceivable that at some time all persons over the age of 18 might be required to file a return, perhaps under the stimulus of a "negative income tax." Actually, inflation and aging of the population act to increase the proportion of filers in the population, as does expansion of social security coverage or any other official listings that enter one on a governmental roll. A number of the files now in current use among the states for estimating populations through regression equations, driver's licenses, for example, can also be used in the way the Census Bureau uses IRS records.

Though the Bureau of the Census itself stresses the problems associated with the use of official records and downplays its own estimates, the fact is, they are quite good for places of 10,000 or more population; indeed, they are better than any that formerly were possible. However, one must be aware that even though compared to a census or a survey, the Administrative Records Procedures are relatively inexpensive, the reduction in cost may be balanced by a reduction in accuracy. The accuracy of the Administrative Records Procedures is affected by the precision with which records can be coded to a constant boundaried area and the representativeness of the records.

However, problems associated with the use of official records at the national and state levels have as yet hardly been explored, and as they become better known, the use of these records will be expanded and the records may be modified with estimation of population and population characteristics in mind. It is doubtless true that a review of federal and state records with a view of eliminating duplication and improving their general usefulness would quickly pay for itself. These records have been independently mandated and developed by bureaus that have little or no contact with each other and no thought except for their own purposes. At the federal level and increasingly at the state level, the use of administrative records for purposes other than those for which they were originally intended is certain to increase, and IRS and other administrative records will continue to be a main source for estimates of migration.

A major suggestion for improvement has been made by Goldsmith and his colleagues. Starting out by using reasoning similar to that utilized for the private synthetic models pictured by Francese that different types of social areas tend to change in different but characteristic ways, they classify areas into several types and show that better estimates are possible when the different types of areas are treated separately. This is analogous to the component method of estimating population where different methods are used for estimating different segments of the population. Goldsmith and his colleagues extend this procedure from different types of people to different types of areas. They are careful, after reviewing their results, to point out that social area cohorts do not necessarily have a uniting direction of change; rather, tract cohorts most likely have a restricted set of potential directions of change. Thus, with social area analysis, particularly if density information is available, it is possible to determine those areas that should be relatively easy to estimate with quick and cheap methods. This restricts the use of more involved and more expensive methods to those areas that are difficult to estimate. The change in social area cohorts between 1970 and 1980 might serve as a preliminary basis for monitoring the direction of small area social change. Once areas are clearly delineated as to directions of change, different techniques may be applied to different types of areas and grand totals obtained by summing the various results. Furthermore, the delineation of areas by social type opens the way to a stratified sampling of areas, thus reducing a troublesome kind of bias that existed for the private synthetic model.

Throughout the conference it was emphasized that there is no one best method of estimating population and it characteristics. Sometimes one method is better than another; at other times, the reverse is true. Furthermore, we may want to use one method for one type of area or for one component of the population and others for other types of areas or population components. As yet we are poorly prepared to decide among estimation procedures or to tailor them for the group and area in question. This, however, can be resolved by research and experience and by learning how best to delineate social areas and use them as geographic components of the estimation process in a way analogous to the way we treat components of the population separately.

The ultimate, of course, is the complex, continuously updated model based upon probabilities of individual behavior that has been pioneered by David Birch and his associates. Expensive and time consuming in its development, it appears to be the most soundly based of the many complex models that were designed to indicate and project population characteristics and other changes in metropolitan areas. No other such model has been so extensively applied and continually improved. It has now been in operation in several cities and in one state, and will receive a crucial test as the results of the 1980 Census become available.

Clearly the testing of this model is necessary, and the model deserves it. On the one hand, its potential to accurately estimate short-term and long-term behavior makes it a valuable monitoring and need assessment tool in spite of its massive data requirement. On the other hand, many large-scale models that simulate behavior have been shown not only to utilize questionable surrogates for independent dimensions but more importantly, they have a very poor record of performance.

If it passes the test and if there is further development of its graphic presentations, there should be a general acceptance in states and large cities. The system is no longer costly in view of the results expected and can be operated by people with no more than readily available computer and statistical training. The Birch model, of course, is tied to a local area, depends on massive inputs of local data, and will not substitute for procedures that are used nationally.

One final issue must be faced. Do we need estimates for small areas such as census tracts, and can we make reasonable estimates for such areas? The answer to the first question has already been given: Estimates for small areas are necessary for all sorts of planning, are essential for required environmental statements, and are necessary for epidemiological and other investigations. The answer to the second question is that we can make estimates for small areas, but we must realize that as the size of the area decreases the relative error will increase. Doubtless we can reduce that error as we learn to classify areas by social type and choose the best methods of estimate for that type of area. Estimates can now be made that are within tolerable limits; those given by the Bureau of the Census for even the smallest places were not at all bad, when absolute as well as relative error is considered. Initial reports from a comparison of estimates and population counts in Minnesota, a state which has pioneered in the use of state and local records and which has emphasized cooperation with localities, indicates a surprisingly good agreement between estimates and counts, years after the census. There is much to learn, but the future is bright, and today's indications are that surveys and estimations will continue to substitute for expensive and resisted quinquennial censuses.

For such endeavors the computer is an ally, though sometimes a dangerous one. With the computer we can store, retrieve, and organize mountains of data accurately and at low cost, and sometimes make them comprehensible. In this regard, the graphic capacities of a computer are almost as valuable as its ability to accept and turn out numbers. In the not-too-distant future, small but powerful computers will be relatively cheap, and we will have a large cadre of people prepared to use and misuse them. The possibilities of using symptomatic data and the easy handling of regressions and matrices with many terms are encouraging if somewhat frightening. For those who have trouble envisioning a model as complex as that developed by Birch and his associates, the future, though bright, is not without clouds.

REFERENCES

KLAY, W. E. (1974) "A comparative analysis of Florida county commissioners: attitudes and perceptions about local population changes: some political, demographic, and economic dimensions." M.A. thesis, University of Georgia.
RICHARDSON, J. D. [ed.] (1969) Compilation of the Messages and Papers of the Presidents 1789-1897, 8: 203.
U.S. Bureau of the Census (1976) Historical Statistics of the United States: Colonial Times to 1970, 6: 1085. Washington, DC: Government Printing Office.
——— (1906) Special Report: Supplementary Analysis and Derivative Tables, 12th Census of the United States, 1900. Washington, DC: Government Printing Office.

Appendix A
The Contributions of C. Horace Hamilton

Gladys K. Bowles

In an article published in 1962, C. Horace Hamilton made the following comments that have particular relevance to small area estimation:

> The need and demand for projections of populations of states, counties, communities, and other small areas have increased greatly during the past few years. Such projections are thought to be the *sine qua non,* as a base, for planning economic and social development—both public and private.

> Even though the basic forces affecting future population trends cannot be accurately evaluated, projections are considered to be useful. Even though his vision may be limited, man has always found it necessary and profitable to peer as far into the future as possible in all phases of action and living. This peering into the future is a continuous process which alternates between the making of adjustments, taking actions, and in the making of more projections, and in the modification of adjustments, actions, and in plans for new actions. Thus, because the future cannot be foretold with high reliability, a great deal of social, economic, and personal "waste" and frustrations occur. The making and improvement of projections is one method that man has of reducing, but not of completely eliminating, waste and frustration. For this reason, projections of one kind or another will continue as long as man, his culture, and his society are what they are [Hamilton and Perry, 1962: 163, 164].

215

In considering C. Horace Hamilton's contributions to small area estimation, I present in this chapter a summary overview of his career rather than selecting three or four items for more intensive consideration. In this way we can see the evolving nature of his work, how it corresponded to the interests of the institutions that employed him, and what some of the prevailing problems and needs for information were in the society in which he operated. Changing emphases within the major disciplines to which he was attached can also be noted as well as expanding individual interests and concerns.

In the early years, along with other rural sociologists with a research orientation, Hamilton studied institutions within the rural society. His first published work related to the role of the church in rural community life in Virginia in 1929. In subsequent years, he issued publications on black churches, farmer's clubs, community organizations, and agriculture and rural life in general.

Throughout his career his association with Land Grant Universities provided the stimulus and support for studies of farm institutions and problems. Among his research concerns were tenancy practices, relief (as welfare was termed then), rental agreements, mechanization, livestock leases, standards and levels of living, education and income deficiencies, bureaucratic entities designed to alleviate farm problems, and the effects of war on farm labor needs and practices.

Very early in his career, because of the association of Land Grant Universities with the U.S. Department of Agriculture (USDA), he became involved in the development of farm population estimates and components of change from one year to the next for Texas, and later North Carolina. This is one of the early examples of the uses of survey data, along with information from other sources, in the production of postcensal population estimates for small areas. The survey schedules and sample designs were crude and the estimating procedures based on judgment and opinion as much as on statistical techniques and precision. Nevertheless, the results documented sweeping changes that were occurring in the agricultural sector for small areas within these states. The development of more sophisticated techniques also stemmed from this early work.

Study of the determinants and concomitants of each of the components of population change and structure became an integral part of Hamilton's professional endeavors. Fertility, mortality, and migration were, of course, basic areas of investigation, but he also considered the effects of marriage rates, life-cycle stages, and other associated complex relationships on current and future population growth or decline. Many of these relationships could only be studied with newly developed or adapted mathematical or statistical techniques. Topography, normal equations, actuarial rates, ordinal variables, and life tables all received attention. Sampling frames and questionnaires were designed and used in state and local surveys to obtain information for program and policy development and as input in the legislative process.

Also early in his career, Hamilton pursued comments made by O. E. Baker, a geographer with the USDA and University of Maryland, on a technique by which residual estimates of net migration could be developed by relating age cohorts from one decennial census to the next, taking survivorship and census errors into account. With a graduate student colleague, F. L. Henderson, he developed the census-survival ratio technique for estimating net migration and demonstrated its usefulness with North Carolina data for the 1920-1930 decade. The application and refinement of this technique continued throughout his career. He did estimates for three decades for North Carolina, for the Tennessee Valley Authority states for one decade, and for the rural or farm populations for a number of areas and time periods. Much of our knowledge of patterns of migration by ascribed characteristics, such as age, sex, race, and ethnicity, stemmed from this research. Many methodological articles were published and other people applied his methods to data for other states and eventually for all counties of the United States.

Later he demonstrated that the census-survival technique could be applied to social as well as to demographic characteristics, adding to our knowledge of the relationships between achieved characteristics (such as education) and migration. His research extended beyond North Carolina rural and farm populations to the South, other regions, and the nation as a whole.

Studies of population trends were also important in these years, and continued to the end of Hamilton's active career. At first he dealt with special populations—North Carolina and its counties, Appalachia, rural blacks, people in certain occupations. His last publication was a 3-volume work that placed North Carolina's current (1970) population structure, changes, and the like in a historical perspective. Extensive information was included on family formation and disruption, and on life-cycle events, as well as on trends in fertility, mortality by cause, and migration to, from, and within the state. Also covered were changes in the labor force, occupation and industry, agricultural trends and farm population, income and levels of living, school enrollment and educational attainment, population projections, and implications for population policy. The breadth of his knowledge of the demography and sociology of the North Carolina population was readily apparent in this outstanding work.

In addition to his other interests, Hamilton became actively concerned about health, medical, and related services and needs in about 1945, and for ten years did much research in these areas. He researched size, occupancy, deaths in, and service needs of hospitals in North Carolina, other parts of the South, and in the nation. He studied general health and medical needs, insurance (voluntary and otherwise) and related matters, not only in North Carolina, but in the Appalachians, and Wisconsin. The prevalence of chronic and other illnesses in rural North Carolina was investigated. Using demographic data he pointed out the need for family planning services in North Carolina. He made studies of the distribution of medical students and progress in health care in various parts of the state. He demonstrated that mortality rates could be used to measure health care needs and progress.

Population projections became a primary interest for Hamilton around 1958 as the society became as concerned in what the future might bring as in what had happened in the past. He did projections for his state of the future total population and its probable structure under given assumptions and made a number of sets of projections of college enrollment and other educational matters. In this period he made what I consider to be another major contribution of particular relevance to small area population estimation. "A Short Method of Projecting Population by Age from One Decade to Another" (Hamilton and Perry, 1962) may well be a challenge to other projectors to reduce methodological complexities that do not add to the reliability of results.

This article contains statements on the need for projections and the place of assumptions in projection methods. It was a major contribution in its time, although it was not the first on this technique. Reference is made in the article to an earlier use by two vital statisticians in England in 1911, and by T. Lynn Smith, who used the method in 1939 in estimating the number of aged persons by states in 1940. Essentially, the method relies on recent past experiences to make projections a decade ahead, for the parts of a total, in his case age groups, when the total is the desired figure. He said:

> Projections by age, from a methodological point of view, should provide more accurate estimates of the *total population of small areas*, because such projections take into consideration not only the effect of the age distribution, but also age-specific rates of natality, mortality, and migration. The superiority of projections by age is analogous to the superiority of age-specific mortality and fertility rates over crude rates [Hamilton and Perry, 1962: 163].

From his carefully documented and illustrated work an appraisal can quickly be made of the strengths and weaknesses of the method. Projections from 1960 to 1970 were presented for the white male population of North Carolina and eighteen age groups. I recently compared the projections to the 1970 published census data. The "Short Method . . ." underestimated the total by less than 50,000, or 2.5 percent below the 1970

Census figure. Not a bad projection by any standards, even though the projections for some individual age groups were not that good. For 9 of the 16 groups for which comparison can be made with the 1970 Census, the differences were 5 percent or less. The 7 age groups that differed by larger percentages were primarily those in which it is more difficult to predict human behavior from the experience of the recent past. Children under 5 were overestimated by nearly one-quarter, as the fertility experience of the 1950-1960 decade did not carry over into the next. (Also, the implicit underenumeration adjustment may have been too high.) And carrying forward the 1950-1960 experience underestimated the number of males in the prime migration ages as North Carolina turned from a moderate to heavy loser to a small or moderate gainer in terms of migration in many of these age groups. The other age group with a large difference between the projections and the 1970 enumerated figure was the 60-64 group where misreporting of age makes census figures suspect and changes in retirement practices make reliable projections difficult.

Nevertheless, I think Hamilton's point was well made that projections of a *total* could stem from making estimates of parts of that total, even though relying solely on the experience of the recent past led to some substantial underestimates in certain age groups.

In considering Hamilton's contributions to the subject of small area estimation, I think the most relevant are his use of survey materials along with those from other sources in the development of estimates, his use of vital statistics sources and other administrative records for clues to changes that were occurring and might be expected to continue or diverge in the future, his development and refinement of a technique for estimating the migration component of population change, and his many methodological statements. Of considerable value to all of us is the care he took to document his work, point out limitations as well as strengths, develop and publish measures of errors that stem from the estimation techniques involved, and his generosity in assisting other researchers whether or not they were involved in matters of primary interest to him. In addition, I recommend to you the entire body of his work. There are nuggets of current significance in a brief agriculturally oriented article as well as in a formal methodological treatise. There is historical information and insight about the future. There is simplicity and clarity of presentation that more of us should try to emulate.

It is fitting that this monograph should be dedicated to the memory of C. Horace Hamilton, rural sociologist, demographer, and scholar.

REFERENCE

HAMILTON, C. H. and J. PERRY (1962) "A short method for projecting population by age from one decennial census to another." Social Forces 41 (December): 163-170.

Appendix B
Bibliography of C. Horace Hamilton

CONTENTS

Part I: Classified List of Publications and Papers, 1926-1965
Charles Horace Hamilton, Ph.D.

RESEARCH BULLETINS, MONOGRAPHS, AND CHAPTERS IN BOOKS

(1) (with W. E. Garnett) *The Role of the Church in Rural Community Life in Virginia.* Virginia Ag. Exp. Sta. Bulletin 267, 191 pages, June 1929.

(2) *Religious Education in Relation to Rural Life in Virginia.* Virginia Council of Religious Education, Bridgewater, VA, 33 pages, 14 figures, 1929.

(3) (with John M. Ellison) *The Negro Church in Rural Virginia.* Virginia Ag. Exp. Sta. Bulletin 273, 40 pages, June 1930.

(4) *Rural-Urban Migration in North Carolina, 1920-1930.* North Carolina Ag. Exp. Sta. Bulletin 295, 85 pages, 27 Figures, February 1934.

(5) A Study of Certain Human and Social Factors in Relation to Soil Erosion and Its Control. A book length research report for the Tennessee Valley Authority, Knoxville, Tenn., 177 pages, 35 photographs, 9 maps, 8 charts, 1935. (unpublished)

(6) *Recent Changes in the Social and Economic Status of Farm Families in North Carolina.* North Carolina Ag. Exp. Sta. Bulletin 309, 180 pages, 59 figures, May 1937.

(7) (with B. W. Forster, R.E.L. Greene, and Selz C. Mayo) *Farm Manpower Situation in North Carolina.* North Carolina Ag. Exp. Sta. Bulletin 340, 29 pages, June 1943.

(8) (with Selz C. Mayo) *Rural Population Problems in North Carolina: Population Growth, 1790-1940.* North Carolina Ag. Exp. Sta. Technical Bulletin 76, 58 pages, August 1943.

(9) (with G. W. Forster, R.E.L. Greene, and Selz C. Mayo) *Farm Labor Problems, 1944.* North Carolina Ag. Exp. Sta. Bulletin 344, 24 pages, May 1944.

(10) (with staff of the Commission on Hospital Care) *Hospital Resources and Needs.* The Report of the Michigan Hospital Survey, W. K. Kellogg Foundation, 172 pages, 14 charts, 1946.

(11) Social Implications of the Family Farm. Contribution to *Family Farm Policy*, pp. 110-113. University of Chicago Press, 1947.

(12)   (with staff of the Commission on Hospital Care) *Hospital Care in the United States.* The Commonwealth Fund, Chapters 11, 14, 15, 16, 18, 19, 20, 21, and 29, 1947.

(13)   (with Clarence Poe and the North Carolina Hospital and Medical Care Commission) *Hospital and Medical Care for All Our People.* (privately published by the authors) Raleigh, N.C., 116 pages, 21 figures, 1947.

(14)   Retirement and Social Security. Chapter 7 of *Time for Action— West Virginia Public Schools,* pp. 149-178. A Survey Report published by Division of Surveys and Field Services, George Peabody College for Teachers, Nashville, Tenn., 1956.

(15)   (with Herbert A. Aurbach) *What's Happening to North Carolina Farms and Farmers?* North Carolina Ag. Exp. Sta. Bulletin 407, 48 pages, 48 figures, 1958.

(16)   Health and Health Services. Chapter 14 in *The Southern Appalachian Region, A Survey,* pp. 217-244. Thomas R. Ford (ed.) Lexington: University of Kentucky Press, 1962.

(17)   (with Josef Perry) 1980 Population Projections for North Carolina Counties. In cooperation with North Carolina Department of Conservation and Development, Division of Community Planning, 230 pages, October 1963.

(18)   Educational Selectivity of Migration from Farm to Urban and to Other Nonfarm Communities. Chapter 7 in *Mobility and Mental Health,* pp. 166-195. Mildren B. Kantor (ed.) Charles B. Thomas, publisher, 1965.

(19)   Continuity and Change in Southern Migration. The School of Agriculture and Alumni Lecture for 1964. North Carolina State University, May 2, 1964. Published as Chapter 3 in *Continuity and Change in the South,* pp. 53-78. John McKinney and Edgar Thompson (eds.) Durham, NC: Duke University Press, 1965.

SCIENTIFIC PAPERS AND POPULAR ARTICLES

(20)   What the Church is Doing in Behalf of the Rural Standards of Living in Virginia. *Bulletin of the Virginia Polytechnic Institute Proceedings of the 1929 Institute of Rural Affairs,* 23: 111-123, January 1930.

(21) Some Factors Affecting the Size of Rural Groups in Virginia. *The American Journal of Sociology*, 36(3): 423-434, November 1930.

(22) A Statistical Index of Topography. *Social Forces*, 9(2): 204-205, December 1930.

(23) Rural Community Organization. *N.C. State Angriculturist*, pp. 2-3 February 1933. Also in leading North Carolina daily newspapers.

(24) The Algebraic Derivation of the Normal Equations Involved in Multiple and Partial Correlation. *Journal of the American Statistical Association*, 28: 204-205, June 1933.

(25) The Natural Increase of Population in North Carolina. *North Carolina State Agriculturist*, p. 11, November 1933.

(26) Research in Rural Institutions. *Scope and Method*, Bulletin 18, Social Science Research Council, Part II and pp. 73-112, 1933.

(27) Farmers' Clubs. Research project outline. *Scope and Method*, Bulletin 12, Social Science Research Council, John D. Black (ed.), pp. 76-82, 1933.

(28) Rural-Urban Migration in the Tennesee Valley Between 1920 and 1930. *Social Forces*, 13(1): 57-64, October 1934.

(29) Break the Backbone of the Tenant System. *Rural America*, 12: 3-5, October 1934.

(30) (with Robin M. Williams) Factors Related to Farm Tenancy in North Carolina. *Journal of Farm Economics*, 16(4): 714-716, October 1934.

(31) The Status and Future of Farm Tenantry in the South. Read before the Southern Economic Society, Duke University, 1935. *Commercial Fertilizer Yearbook for 1936*, 6 pages.

(32) The Annual Rate of Departure of Rural Youths from Their Parental Homes. *Rural Sociology*, 1(2): 164-179, June 1936.

(33) (with Charles P. Loomis) Family Life Cycle Analysis. *Social Forces*, 15: 225-231, December 1936.

(34) The Trend of the Marriage Rate in Rural North Carolina. *Rural Sociology*, 1(4): 452-471, December 1936.

(35) Trends in the Fertility of Married Women of Different Social Groups in Certain Rural Areas of North Carolina. *Rural Sociology*, 2(2): 192-203, June 1937.

(36) Farm Rental Contracts and Agreements. *Texas Agriculturist Journal*, 1: 2-3, 9, 18, 20, January 1938.

(37) Texas Farm Tenure Activities. *Journal of Land and Public Utility Economics*, 14: 331-333, August 1938.

(38) An Experimental Farm Rental Agreement. *Rural America*, 16: 7-8, November 1938.

(39) An Improved Farm Rental Contract. *Rural America*, 17: 14-15, March 1939.
(40) The Social Effects of the Recent Trends in Mechanization of Agriculture. *Rural Sociology*, 4(1): 3-25, March 1939.
(41) Steel Mules. *Land Policy Review*, 2(2): 1-7, March-April 1939.
(42) Specific Legislation Affecting Farm Tenure Which Should be Encouraged. *Southwestern Social Science Quarterly*, 20(4): 1-10, March 1940.
(43) (with F. M. Henderson) Migration from North Carolina Farms. *University of North Carolina News Letter*, 29(4), 1943.
(44) A Master Sample for Enumeration in Rural Areas. *Rural Sociology*, 9(1): 66-67, March 1944.
(45) Comparing Two Questionnaire Surveys of Farm Population. *Rural Sociology*, 9(1): 62-66, March 1944.
(46) Less Manpower—More Production. North Carolina Ag. Exp. Sta. *Research and Farming*, 2: 11-12, April 1944.
(47) A Critical Review of Hagood's Rural Level of Living Indexes for Counties of the United States, 1940. *Rural Sociology*, 9(2): 184-187, June 1944.
(48) Use of the Survival Rate Method in Measuring Net Migration. *Journal of the American Statistical Association*, 39: 197-206, June 1944.
(49) (with Richard L. Anderson) Derivation of Formulas for Use in Computing *True* Simple Interest Rates. North Carolina Ag. Exp. Sta. Technical Bulletin 80, pp. 24-28, September 1944.
(50) Population Density and the Size of Hospital Communities. American Hospital Association, *Hospitals*, 19(11): 57-60, November 1945.
(51) Distribution of Medical College Students by Residence. *Journal of the Association of American Medical Colleges*, pp. 3-7, January 1946.
(52) Normal Occupancy Rate in the General Hospital. American Hospital Association, *Hospitals*, 19(12), September 1946.
(53) Planning for Rural Health Centers and Hospitals. North Carolina Ag. Exp. Sta. *Research and Farming*, 5(2): 11-13, January 1947.
(54) Hospitals and Health Centers for the Rural South. A special section of *The South's Health: A Picture with Promise*, Leland Tate (ed.). Hearings on a Study of Agricultural and Economic Problems of the Cotton Belt before the Special Subcommittee on Cotton of the House Committee on Agriculture, 1947.
(55) Some Applications of Population Research to Welfare Problems. Presented to the Texas Population Conference, April 1947.

Published by Texas Ag. Exp. Sta., Misc. Pub. 12, pp. 9-11, November 1947.

(56) Bias and Error in Multiple-Choice Tests. *Psychometrika*, 15(2): 151-168, June 1950.

(57) Some Current Problems in the Development of Rural Sociology. *Rural Sociology*, 15(4): 315-321, December 1950.

(58) Population Pressure and Other Factors Affecting Net Rural-Urban Migration. *Social Forces*, 30(2): 209-215, December 1951.

(59) (with Jacob Siegel) Some Considerations in the Use of the Residual Method of Estimating Net Migration. *Journal of the American Statistical Association*, 47(259): 475-500, September 1952.

(60) Procedures Used in the Preparation of a Medical Service Area Map for North Carolina. *Rural Sociology*, 17(4): 367-370, December 1952.

(61) Ecological and Social Factors in Mortality Variation. *American Eugenics Quarterly*, 2(4): 212-223, December 1955.

(62) Educational Selectivity of Rural-Urban Migration: Preliminary Results of a North Carolina Study. *Proceedings of the 1957 Annual Conference*, Milbank Memorial Foundation, New York, pp. 110-122, 1958.

(63) The Sociology of a Changing Agriculture. *Social Forces*, 37(1): 1-7, March 1958.

(64) Educational Selectivity of Net Migration from the South. *Social Forces*, 38(1): 33-39, October 1959.

(65) The Net Migration Rate: A Methodological Note. *Social Forces*, 38(1): 40-42, October 1959.

(66) (with Selz C. Mayo and Charles W. Pettus) Sources of Variation in the Level of Living of Farm Operators in the United States. *Social Forces*, 39(4): 338-346, May 1961.

(67) Some Problems of Method in Internal Migration Research. *Population Index*, 27(4): 297-307, October 1961.

(68) (with Josef Perry) A Short Method for Projecting Population by Age from One Decennial Census to Another. *Social Forces*, 41(2): 163-170, December 1962.

(69) (with Selz C. Mayo) Now Outnumbering Farm Children—Urban Youngsters. North Carolina Ag. Exp. Sta. *Research and Farming*, 24(2): 4-5, Winter-Spring 1963.

(70) The Addition Theorem and Analysis of Variance in the Case of Correlated Nominal Variates. North Carolina Ag. Exp. Sta. Research Paper 1389, Journal Series, September 15, 1963. (multilithed)

(71) (with Selz C. Mayo) Current Population Trends in the South. Presented at the Annual Meeting of the Southern Sociological Society, Louisville, Ky. *Social Forces*, 42: 77-88, October 1963.

(72) (with Selz C. Mayo) The Rural Negro Population of the South in Transition. *Phylon*, 24: 160-171, 1963.

(73) The Negro Leaves the South. *Demography*, 1: 273-275, 1964.

(74) Comparison of Two Formulas in Making Population Estimates. *Rural Sociology*, 29: 426-431, December 1964.

(75) County Net Migration Rates—Discussion of a Paper by James D. Tarver and William R. Gurley. *Rural Sociology*, 30(1): 13-17, March 1965.

(76) (with Elizabeth M. Suval) Some New Evidence on Educational Selectivity in Migration to and from the South. *Social Forces*, 43(4): 536-547, May 1965.

(77) Practical and Mathematical Considerations in the Formulation and Selection of Migration Rates. *Demography*, 2: 429-443, 1965.

BOOK AND BULLETIN REVIEWS

(78) Book Review of Wilson Gee, *The Social Economics of Agriculture*. (New York: Macmillan, 1932). *Rural America*, 9: 13, April 1933.

(79) Bulletin Review of Harry H. Kohler and Susan Z. Wilder, *Music Appreciation Programs for Rural Schools*. (South Dakota College Extension Service Circular 308). *Winston-Salem Journal and Sentinel, Charlotte Observer* and other state papers, March 6, 1932.

(80) Book Review of R. Clyde White, *Social Statistics*. (New York: Harper & Bros., 1933). *Social Forces*, 12: 308-309, December 1933.

(81) Book Review of C. Warren Thornthwaite, *Internal Migration in the United States*. (Philadelphia: University of Pennsylvania Press, 1934). *Journal of the American Statistical Association*, 30: 765-766, December 1935.

(82) Book Review of Charles S. Johnson, Edwin R. Embree, and W. W. Alexander, *The Collapse of Cotton Tenancy*. (Chapel Hill: Uni-

versity of North Carolina Press, 1935). *Rural Sociology*, 1: 110-112, March 1936.

(83) Book Review of Carter Goodrich, Bushrod W. Allin, and Marion Hayes, *Migration and Planes of Living 1920-1934.* (Philadelphia: University of Pennsylvania Press, 1935). *Rural Sociology*, 1: 524-526, December 1936.

(84) Book Review of Eyler N. Simpson, *The Ejido: Mexico's Way Out.* (Chapel Hill: University of North Carolina Press, 1937). *Journal of Farm Economics*, 19: 963-965, November 1937.

(85) Book Review of Louis I. Dublin and Alfred J. Lotka, *Length of Life: A Study of the Life Table.* (New York: Ronald Press, 1936). *Rural Sociology*, 2: 505, December 1937.

(86) Book Review of J. H. Kolb and Edmund deS. Brunner, *A Study of Rural Society: Its Organization and Changes.* (Boston: Houghton-Mifflin, 1940); Newell L. Sims, *Elements of Rural Sociology.* (New York: Thomas Y. Crowell, 1940); Paul H. Landis, *Rural Life in Process.* (New York: McGraw-Hill, 1940). *Social Forces*, 19: 435-438, March 1941.

(87) Book Review of Margaret J. Hagood, *Statistics for Sociologists.* (New York: Reynal and Hitchcock, 1941); Thomas C. McCormick, *Elementary Social Statistics.* (New York: McGraw-Hill, 1941); Mordecai Ezekiel, *Methods of Correlation Analysis.* (New York: John Wiley, 1941). *Rural Sociology*, 7: 112-113, March 1942.

(88) Book Review of Frank A. Pearson and Kenneth R. Bennett, *Statistical Methods: Applied to Agricultural Economics.* (New York: John Wiley, 1942). *Rural Sociology*, 7: 455-456, December 1942.

(89) Book Review of John D. Black, *Parity Parity Parity.* (Cambridge, MA: Harvard Committee on Research in the Social Sciences, 1942). *Social Forces*, 21: 241-242, December 1942.

(90) Book Review of Clare Leighton, *Southern Harvest.* (New York: Macmillan, 1942). *Rural Sociology*, 8: 316-317, September 1943.

(91) Bulletin Review of Margaret J. Hagood, *Rural Level of Living Indexes for Counties of the United States, 1940.* (U.S. Department of Agriculture, Bureau of Agricultural Economics, October 1943). *Rural Sociology*, 9: 184-186, June 1944.

(92) Bulletin Review of Eleanor H. Bernert, *Volume and Composition of Net Migration From the Rural-Farm Population, 1930-40, for the United States.* (U.S. Department of Agriculture, Bureau of Agricultural Economics, January 1944). *Rural Sociology*, 9: 186-187, June 1944.

(93) Bulletin Review of Earle E. Muntz, *Proposals for Health, Old Age and Unemployment Insurance: A Comparison of the 1943 and 1945 Wagner-Murray Bills.* (New York: American Enterprise Association).

(94) Critique of Bell Boone Beard, *Testing Sociology Instruction. Social Forces*, 24: 73-74, October 1945.

(95) Book Review of Charles P. Loomis, *Studies of Rural Social Organization in the United States, Latin America and Germany.* (East Lansing, MI: State College Book Store, 1945). *American Sociological Review*, 11: 132-133, February 1946.

(96) Book Review of Rupert B. Vance, *All These People.* (Chapel Hill: University of North Carolina Press, 1946). *Rural Sociology*, 11: 285-286, September 1946.

(97) Book Review of Granville Hicks, *Small Town.* (New York: Macmillan, 1946); Wayland J. Hayes, *The Small Community Looks Ahead.* (New York: Harcourt Brace & Co., 1947); Jean and Jess Ogden, *Small Communities in Action.* (New York: Harper & Bros., 1946). *Land Policy Review*, 10: 24-25, Summer-Fall 1947.

(98) Book Review of Bernard J. Stern, *Medical Services by Government.* (New York: Commonwealth Fund, 1946); Harry S. Mustard, *Government in Public Health.* (New York: Commonwealth Fund, 1945). *American Journal of Sociology*, 53: 75-76, July 1947.

(99) Book Review of Louis I. Dublin and Alfred J. Lotka, *The Money Value of a Man.* (New York: Ronald Press, 1946). *Rural Sociology*, 12: 326-327, September 1947.

(100) Book Review of William Ransom Hogan, *The Texas Republic—A Social and Economic History.* (Norman: University of Oklahoma Press, 1946). *Rural Sociology*, 12: 327, September 1947.

(101) Book Review of Otis Durant Duncan, *Social Research on Health.* (New York: Social Science Research Council, 1946). *Journal of Political Economics*, 55: 579-580, December 1947.

(102) Book Review of Frederick D. Mott, M.D., and Milton I. Raemer, M.D., M.P.H., *Rural Health and Medical Care.* (New York: McGraw-Hill, 1948). *American Sociological Review*, 13: 790-791, December 1948.

(103) Book Review of John D. Durand, *The Labor Force in the United States, 1890-1960.* (New York: Social Science Research Council, 1948). *Journal of Economic History*, 9: 120-121, May 1949.

(104) Book Review of Garland A. Hendricks, *Biography of a Country Church.* (Nashville: Rodman Press, 1950). *Rural Sociology*, 16: 82-83, March 1951.

(105) Bulletin Review of Barbara B. Reagan and Evelyn Grossman, *Rural Levels of Living in Lee and Jones Counties, Mississippi, 1945, and a Comparison of Two Methods of Data Collection.* (Washington, DC: U.S. Department of Agriculture Agricultural Information Bulletin 41, October 1951). *Journal of the American Statistical Association,* 47: 702-704, December 1952.

(106) Book Review of Kingsley Davis, *The Population of India and Pakistan.* (Princeton, NJ: Princeton University Press, 1951). *Rural Sociology,* 17: 382-383, December 1952.

(107) Book Review of Lewis J. Moorman, M.D., *Pioneer Doctor.* (Norman: University of Oklahoma Press, 1951). *Rural Sociology,* 17: 392-393, December 1952.

(108) Bulletin Review of John F. Thaden, *Distribution of Doctors of Medicine and Osteopaths in Michigan Communities.* (Michigan Ag. Exp. Sta. Special Bulletin 370, June 1951). *Rural Sociology,* 17: 398-399, December 1952.

(109) Book Review of Margaret J. Hagood and Daniel O. Price, *Statistics for Sociologists.* (New York: Henry Holt, 1952). *Rural Sociology,* 18: 275-277, September 1953.

(110) Book Review of Morris H. Hansen, William M. Hurwitz, and William G. Madow, *Sample Survey Methods and Theory, Vol. I: Methods and Applications; Vol. II: Theory.* (New York: John Wiley: 1953). *Rural Sociology,* 19: 200-201, June 1954.

(111) Book Review of W. Allen Wallis and Harry V. Roberts, *Statistics: A New Approach.* (Glencoe, IL: Free Press, 1956). *Social Forces,* 35: 290-291, March 1957.

(112) Book Review of Kenneth D. S. Baldwin, *The Niger Agricultural Project.* (Cambridge, MA: Harvard University Press, 1957). *South Atlantic Quarterly,* 58: 308-310, Spring 1959.

(113) Book Review of Eleanor H. Bernert, *America's Children.* (New York: John Wiley, 1958). *Rural Sociology,* 24: 61, March 1959.

(114) Book Review of Maurice Halbwachs, *Population and Society.* (Glencoe, IL: Free Press, 1960). *Social Forces* 40: 183, December 1961.

RESEARCH PROGRESS REPORTS AND RELATED PAPERS

(115) Handbook, Outline, Theory and Objectives of the Study of the Economic Significance of Different Leasing Systems in Texas, 1936.

(116) Texas Farm Population Changes During 1936. *Progress Report 453*, Texas Ag. Exp. Sta., July 1937.

(117) Texas Farm Population During 1937. *Research Report*, Texas Ag. Exp. Sta., July 1938.

(118) Statistics on Farm Tenancy in Texas. *Progress Report 580*, Texas Ag. Exp. Sta., December 1938.

(119) An Experimental Farm Rental Agreement. *Progress Report 478*, Texas Ag. Exp. Sta., 1937. (revised, 1939)

(120) Farm Population Changes in Texas During 1938. *Progress Report 644*, Texas Ag. Exp. Sta., October 1939.

(121) (with Jay Wakeley) Some Effects of the War Upon the Farm Labor Situation in North Carolina. *Research Report*, August 1, 1942.

(122) (with Selz C. Mayo) Farm Labor Available in an Urban Center, Washington, N.C. *Progress Report RS-1*, North Carolina Ag. Exp. Sta., 1943.

(123) Farm Population Changes in North Carolina During 1943. *Progress Report RS-2*, North Carolina Ag. Exp. Sta., April 1944.

(124) (with Mary E. Halloway and Margaret M. Cole) Rural North Carolina Needs Doctors. North Carolina Ag. Exp. Sta. *Research and Farming*, October 1944.

(125) The Need for Rural Hospitals. North Carolina Ag. Exp. Sta. *Research and Farming*, January 1945.

(126) (with M. R. Chambers and Staff) Hospital and Medical Care Facilities in North Carolina. *Progress Report RS-4*, North Carolina Ag. Exp. Sta., 90 pages, 41 charts, 52 tables, summary, and references, February 1945.

(127) Rural Health and Medical Service in North Carolina. *Progress Report RS-9*, North Carolina Ag. Exp. Sta., August 1950.

(128) Chronic Illness—An Increasing Burden on Rural People. *Progress Report RS-10*, North Carolina Ag. Exp. Sta., May 1951.

(129) Working Together for Better Health and Medical Service in Rural North Carolina. *Progress Report RS-12A*, North Carolina Ag. Exp. Sta., July 1951.

(130) A Study of the Need for Several Small Hospitals in Rural Wake County, North Carolina. *Progress Report RS-15*, North Carolina Ag. Exp. Sta., September 1952.

(131) Net Migration To and From North Carolina and North Carolina Counties From 1940 to 1950. *Progress Report RS-18*, North Carolina Ag. Exp. Sta., September 1953.

(132) (with Donald G. Hay) Enrollment in Voluntary Health Insurance in North Carolina, 1953. *Progress Report RS-23*, North Carolina Ag. Exp. Sta., September 1954.

(133) (with Donald G. Hay) Acceptance of Voluntary Health Insurance in Four Rural Communities of Haywood County, North Caro-

lina, 1953. *Progress Report RS-24*, North Carolina Ag. Exp. Sta., September 1954.

(134) Health Progress in North Carolina From 1940 to 1950 as Measured by Age Adjusted Mortality Rates. *Progress Report RS-21*, North Carolina Ag. Exp. Sta., September 1954.

(135) North Carolina Abridged Life Tables, by Color and Sex, 1949-1951, Showing Expected Future Lifetime by Quartiles. Showing Comparison with 1925 and 1940. *Progress Report RS-22*, North Carolina Ag. Exp. Sta., September 1954.

(136) North Carolina's Expected 1960 Population by Age, Color and Sex. *Progress Report RS-33*, North Carolina Ag. Exp. Sta., 1958.

(137) Health and Health Services in the Southern Appalachians: A Source Book. *Progress Report RS-35*, North Carolina Ag. Exp. Sta., September 1959.

(138) (with Selz C. Mayo) Hospitals and Hospital Services in North Carolina: A Source Book. *Progress Report RS-37*, North Carolina Ag. Exp. Sta., October 1960.

(139) (with Selz C. Mayo) Physicians and Characteristics of Physicians and Other Health Personnel in North Carolina. *Progress Report RS-38*, North Carolina Ag. Exp. Sta., November 1960.

(140) *Distribution and Characteristics of Physicians in Wisconsin: A Source Book of Tables*. Department of Rural Sociology, University of Wisconsin, 1960.

(141) *Hospital and Hospital Services Areas in Wisconsin: A Source Book of Tables*. Department of Rural Sociology, University of Wisconsin, 1960.

(142) Southern Appalachians: Greatly in Need of Health Services. North Carolina Ag. Exp. Sta. *Research and Farming*, 19: 3-4, Winter-Spring, 1961.

(143) By 1980 North Carolina Colleges May Enroll Between 123,897 and 174,726 Students. *North Carolina Public School Bulletin*, February 1962.

(144) Projections of Fall Enrollment in North Carolina Colleges and Universities, 1962-1980. *Progress Report RS-41*, North Carolina Ag. Exp. Sta., February 1962.

(145) Community Colleges for North Carolina: A Study of Need, Location, and Service Areas. *Progress Report RS-42*, North Carolina Ag. Exp. Sta., September 1962. (abridged edition)

(146) Community Colleges for North Carolina, A Study of Need, Location, and Service Areas. *Progress Report RS-42X*, North Carolina Ag. Exp. Sta., December 1962. (unabridged edition)

(147) North Carolina Abridged Life Tables by Color and Sex, 1959-1961. *Progress Report RS-44*, North Carolina Ag. Exp. Sta., September 1964.

(148) Projection of Fall Enrollment in North Carolina Colleges and Universities. *Progress Report RS-46*, North Carolina Ag. Exp. Sta., January 1965.

(148a) High School Graduate Projections, North Carolina Counties 1966-1976. *Progress Report RS-48*, North Carolina Ag. Exp. Sta., December 1965.

RADIO ADDRESSES AND INTERVIEWS

(149) The Farmer's Church in Virginia. V.P.I. Radio Station, April 17, 1930.

(150) The Future of the Country Church. V.P.I. Radio Station, May 15, 1930.

(151) Have We Counted the Cost of Rural Emigration? V.P.I. Radio Station, August 20, 1930.

(152) The Need for Recreation in the Country Community. V.P.I. Radio Station, September 1, 1930.

(153) Budget Wisely. WPTF, Raleigh, N.C., January 26, 1933.

(154) Adult Education for Farm People. WPTF, Raleigh, N.C., October 23, 1935.

(155) Social Security for Farm Tenants. WPTF, Raleigh, N.C., November 20, 1935.

(156) Recent Population Trends in North Carolina. WPTF, Raleigh, N.C., December 4, 1935.

(157) The Bankhead-Jones Tenant Land Bill and Experiment Station Study. WTAW, TQN, College Station, Texas, July 26, 1937.

(158) Characteristics of Our Present Leasing Systems. WTAW, College Station, Texas, August 2, 1937.

(159) Farm Rental Contracts and Agreements. WTAW, TQN, College Station, Texas, August 16, 1937.

(160) Texas Farm Population Changes. WTAW, TQN, College Station, Texas, August 16, 1937.

(161) The Migration of Farm Population to Cities. WTAW, TQN, College Station, Texas, June 3, 1938.

(162) An Improved Leasing Contract Will Increase Farm Income. WTAW, TQN, College Station, Texas, May 10, 1938.

(163) Objectives of Farm Tenancy Legislation. WTAW, TQN, College Station, Texas, March 3, 1939.

(164) Farm Mechanization in Texas. WTAW, TQN, College Station, Texas, January 6, 1939.

(165) The Progress of the Farm Tenancy Bill. WTAW, TQN, College Station, Texas, March 17, 1939.

(166) A Survey of Public Opinion on the Farm Tenancy Question. WTAW, TQN, College Station, Texas, March 24, 1939.

(167) The Cost of Medical Service to Farmers. WTAW, TQN, College Station, Texas, March 31, 1939.

(168) National Health Insurance. WNAO, Raleigh, N.C., February 6, 1950.

OTHER PAPERS AND REPORTS

(169) An Analysis of Recorder's Court Cases, Durham, North Carolina, 1922-1926. Institute for Research in Social Science, Chapel Hill, N.C., 1926.

(170) Extent and Types of Juvenile Delinquency and Dependency in Durham, North Carolina, 1926. Institute for Research in Social Science, Chapel Hill, N.C., 1926.

(171) The Church and the Rural Community Research Paper. Virginia Polytechnic Institute, 1928.

(172) Community Development Trends in Relation to Rural Institutions in Virginia. Virginia Polytechnic Institute, 1928.

(173) Needed Adjustments in the Rural Church. Virginia Polytechnic Institute, 1928. Published in the Religious Herald, Richmond, Va., May 24, 1928.

(174) Religion in Blacksburg, Virginia. Virginia Polytechnic Institute, 1928.

(175) The Future of the Country Church. Virginia Polytechnic Institute, 1929.

(176) The Task of the Rural Church. Virginia Polytechnic Institute, 1929. Published in the Religious Herald, Richmond, Va., May 10, 1928, and the Richmond Christian Advocate, July 26, 1928.

(177) The Rural Church. The Presbyterian Survey, 18: 455-458, Richmond, Va., August 1928.

(178) Discoveries in Rural Virginia. Virginia Polytechnic Institute, 1930.

(179) Discovering the Problems of the Rural Church. Virginia Polytechnic Institute, 1930.

(180) What Can Religion and the Organized Church Contribute to the
Well-being of Rural Society? Virginia Polytechnic Institute,
1930.

(181) What Research Can Contribute to the Selection of Subject Matter
for Introductory Courses in Social Science. Read before the
Virginia Social Science Assn., Lynchburg, Va., 1929. Abstract
published in the Proceedings of the Association, 1930.

(182) (with G. W. Forster) Trends in Farm Population and Agriculture.
North Carolina Farm Business, 2: 3-4, October 1931.

(183) The Field of Rural Sociology and Its Relation to Agricultural
Economics. North Carolina State College, 1931.

(184) Child Labor on Farms in North Carolina with Especial Reference
to Over-Production and School Attendance. Read before the
North Carolina Conference on Social Service, Durham, N.C.,
1932.

(185) The Contribution of Rural Sociology to the Church. Read before a
joint meeting of the American Farm Economic Association and
the American Sociological Society, December 1932.

(186) Interpretation of Social Theories from the Greeks to the Present,
with Special Reference to the Community. Ph.D. Examination,
University of North Carolina, 1932.

(187) Some Factors Affecting Land Values in North Carolina. Read to
the Land Appraisers School at State College, North Carolina,
1934.

(188) The Outlook for Rural Sociology in the South. Read to the Rural
Sociology Section of the American Sociological Society,
December 1934.

(189) The Relation of the Agricultural Adjustment Program to Rural
Relief Needs in North Carolina. Research Progress Report,
November 22, 1935.

(190) Farm Tenancy: An Old Problem Comes Back. Departmental Paper,
1935.

(191) How to Live at Home and Yet Enjoy Comfortable Living Standards. *News and Observer*, February 4, 1935, and a number of
other North Carolina newspapers. Departmental Paper, 1935.

(192) Negro Teachers' Salaries in North Carolina, 1933-1934. A report
for the State Board of Education and the North Carolina Inter-
racial Commission, 1935.

(193) Significant Developments in Social Research Under the Federal
Emergency Relief Administration. Read to the Rural Sociology
Section of the American Sociological Society, December 1935.

(194)   The Size of Occupational Groups in North Carolina in Relation to the Problem of Taxation. *News and Observer,* Sunday feature, 1935.

(194a) Birth Rate Declining in North Carolina and the Nation Generally. *News and Observer,* feature article, December 8, 1935.

(195)   A State Farm Tenancy Program. Paper read to the Texas Conference of Social Welfare, April 23, 1937.

(196)   On Federal Farm Tenancy Legislation with Special Reference to the Bankhead Farmers Home Corporation Bill, S-106. Texas Ag. Exp. Sta., 1937.

(197)   Some Social Aspects of Land Tenure in the Southwest. Read to the Southwestern Social Science Association, Dallas, Texas, 1937.

(198)   A Digest of the Farm Tenancy Report of the President's Committee. Prepared for the Director of the Texas Agricultural Experiment Station, 1937.

(199)   Social Aspects of Cotton Culture. Read to Cotton Short Course, Corpus Christi, Texas, May 7, 1938.

(200)   What Farmers Think About Farm Tenancy. Discussion and attitude questionnaire, Texas Ag. Exp. Sta., 1938.

(201)   (with Senator William Corry) The Texas Farm Tenancy Act. A bill introduced by Senator Corry in the Texas Legislature, March 9, 1939.

(202)   Livestock Leases on Cotton Farms. *Farm and Ranch,* Dallas, June 1939.

(203)   The Farm Leasing System of Texas. Abstract. Texas Ag. Exp. Sta., 1939.

(204)   A Survey of Public Opinion on Farm Ownership and Tenancy. Research Report, Texas Ag. Exp. Sta., 1939.

(205)   The Standard of Living of Farm Laborers. Testimony before the Senate Committee on Education and Labor, Washington, D.C., May 1940.

(206)   Charting Areas of Rural Sociological Research in the South. Address, the Southern Conference Seminar on Teaching and Research in Rural Sociology, Blue Ridge, N.C., August 26-30, 1940.

(207)   The Aim and Scope of Land Use Planning: A Sociological Interpretation. Read to the Section on Agricultural Economics and Rural Sociology, Southern Agricultural Workers Association, Atlanta, February 6, 1941.

(208)   Methods of Measuring Levels of Living of Farm Families. North Carolina State College, Raleigh, N.C., 1941.

(209)   (with F. M. Henderson) Migration from North Carolina Farms. *University of North Carolina Newsletter,* February 24, 1943.

(210) Significant Changes in the Agricultural Labor Force of North Carolina. *News and Observer,* April 13, 1943.
(211) The Conservation of Human and Social Values in Rural Life. Presented to the Rural Church Seminar, Duke University, 1943.
(212) Resettlement of Service Men on the Land. Planning Report. North Carolina State College, December 3, 1943.
(213) (with S. H. Hobbs, Jr.) Conclusions and Principles Based on the Farm Foundation Conference on Medical Care and Health Service in Rural Areas in Chicago, Illinois, April 11-13, 1944.
(214) Planning for Rural Medical and Hospital Care. *Farmers Federation News,* August 1944.
(215) Medical Care and Hospital Facilities for Rural People in North Carolina. Report prepared for and presented to the Governor's Commission on Hospital Care, October 11, 1944.
(216) Elements of a State Medical Care Plan. Presented to the Governor's Commission on Hospital and Medical Care, 1944.
(217) Housing in Postwar Rural America. Research Memorandum, North Carolina Ag. Exp. Sta., 1944.
(218) Statement on the Farm Security Administration. Testimony before the U.S. House of Representatives Committee on Agriculture, 1944.
(219) Agriculture, Rural Life and the Church in the Postwar Era. *Methodist Rural Fellowship Special Bulletin 3.* An address at the annual dinner of the Methodist Rural Fellowship, Elgin, Ill., November 17, 1944. Reprinted in *The Christian Rural Fellowship Bulletin 103,* May 1945.
(220) A Series of Newspaper Feature Articles on the Medical Care Needs and Plans for Rural People in North Carolina. Published in the Raleigh *News and Observer,* July 1944 to March 1945.
Article 1: The Need for Group Health Care in Rural Areas.
Article 2: Commercial and Cooperative Medical Care Plans.
Article 3: The Blue Cross Plan.
Article 4: Federal Public Health Insurance.
Article 5: Life and Death in North Carolina.
(221) Land Tenure and Human Welfare in the South of Tomorrow. *Prophetic Religion,* Winter 1945, pp. 75-77.
(222) (with a committee). Rural Medical Needs: Plans. Report of Rural Committee, North Carolina Hospital and Medical Care Commission, *University of North Carolina News Letter,* January 17, 1945.
(223) The Rural Hospital Problem and Size of the Hospital Community. *Hospital Survey News Letter,* Chicago, Ill., October 1945.

(224) Medical Care Needs and Plans for Rural People in North Carolina. A mineographed reprint of five feature newspaper articles, Raleigh *News and Observer,* July 1944 to March 1945.

(225) The Problem of Financing Hospital and Medical Care. Address before the joint session of the Hospital Trustees Institute and the Tri-State Hospital Assembly. Chicago, Ill., May 2, 1946.

(226) The Bed Occupancy Rate in General Hospitals. *Hospital Survey News Letter,* Chicago, Ill., June 1946.

(227) A New Formula for Estimating the Need for General Hospital Beds. *Hospital Survey News Letter,* Chicago, Ill., July 1946.

(228) Guarantees to Security on the Land. Departmental Planning Paper, North Carolina Ag. Exp. Sta., 1947.

(229) Health and Health Insurance for Rural People. Departmental Planning Paper, North Carolina Ag. Exp. Sta., 1947.

(230) Health Leaders Agree on Basic Principles of Medical Insurance. Departmental Paper summarizing the report of the National Health Assembly, North Carolina Ag. Exp. Sta., 1947.

(231) Measuring Need for Rural Hospitals and Clinics. Departmental Research Report, North Carolina Ag. Exp. Sta., 1947.

(232) Recommendations with reference to the annual report of the Bureau of Vital Statistics, North Carolina State Board of Health. North Carolina Ag. Exp. Sta., 1947.

(233) (with a committee) Report of the Committee on Research. Southern Sociological Society, Atlanta, Ga., 1947.

(234) Rural Health, Population Under Survey. North Carolina Ag. Exp. Sta., *Research and Farming,* 6(1), October 1947.

(235) Rural Medical Service and County Lines. Departmental Research Report, North Carolina Ag. Exp. Sta., 1947.

(236) Farm Tenancy Increases in East. 70th Annual Report, North Carolina Ag. Exp. Sta., *Research and Farming,* April 1948.

(237) Sickness in Eastern North Carolina. *The University of North Carolina News Letter,* 35(8), April 1948.

(238) Rural Medical Care. *Better Health for North Carolina,* 2(4), June-July 1948.

(239) Farm Living Level Improves. North Carolina Ag. Exp. Sta., *Research and Farming,* 7(1), July 1948.

(240) How Farm Folks Get Better Hospital and Better Medical Care. *Progressive Farmer,* pp. 12 and 60, October 1948.

(241) Human Resources and Education in North Carolina. Memorandum for the North Carolina Education Commission, North Carolina Ag. Exp. Sta., 1948.

(242) Rural Isolation and Medical Services. Departmental Research Report, North Carolina Ag. Exp. Sta., 1948.

(243) Rural Life and Rural Social Organization. Departmental Planning Memorandum for the School of Agriculture, North Carolina Ag. Exp. Sta., 1948.

(244) The South: 1938-1948. Departmental Paper, North Carolina Ag. Exp. Sta., 1948.

(245) What's Your State Doing About Health and Hospitals? *The Progressive Farmer*, page 27ff., April 1949.

(246) The Farmer Needs a Telephone. Departmental Paper, North Carolina Ag. Exp. Sta., 1950.

(247) Home Environment a Key to Good Health. Departmental Paper, North Carolina Ag. Exp. Sta., 1950.

(248) A Note on "Bias and Error in Multiple Choice Tests." A rejoinder to Samuel B. Lyerly's criticism of Hamilton's paper in *Psychometrika*, 15: 151-168, June 1950.

(249) Many Family Incomes in Wake County Too Low for Good Health Care. Departmental Research Report, North Carolina Ag. Exp. Sta., 1950.

(250) Shotguns and Surveys in the Quest for Better Health. Departmental Paper, North Carolina Ag. Exp. Sta., Winter 1951.

(251) Chronic Illnesses Take a Toll. *Research and Farming*, North Carolina Ag. Exp. Sta., Spring 1951.

(252) Working Together for Better Health and Medical Service in Rural North Carolina. *Progress Report RS-12A*, North Carolina Ag. Exp. Sta., July 1951.

(253) Chronic Illness in a Rural Area. *Chronic Illness News Letter*, 2(9), September 1951.

(254) Progress in Reverse. North Carolina Ag. Exp. Sta., *Research and Farming*, 10 (Progress Report 2), Autumn 1951.

(255) Facts About the Proposed Hospital Bond Election for Wake County. Presented to the County Board of Commissioners, 1951.

(256) (with Selz C. Mayo) The Challenge of Better Community Organization in Rural North Carolina. Report to the North Carolina Agricultural Experiment Station, 1952.

(257) (with James W. Green) The Challenge of Improved Community Housing in North Carolina. Report to the North Carolina Agricultural Experiment Station, 1952.

(258) (with a College Committee, C. Horace Hamilton, Chairman) Group Life and Health Insurance for the Faculty and Employees of North Carolina State College, May 1, 1952.

(259) Two Important Next Steps in a Good Health Program for Rural North Carolina. Statement prepared for the North Carolina Agricultural Experiment Station, August 1952.

(260) Census Statistics on North Carolina Farm Families. North Carolina Agricultural Extension Service, November 1953.

(261) Questionnaire: Health Insurance and Prepayment Plans and Problems with Special Reference to North Carolina Conditions, Needs, Experience and Attitudes. Prepared for a committee of the North Carolina Conference for Social Service, May 1954.

(262) Mortality Trends and Differentials in North Carolina. The Mortality-Vitality Index. Departmental Research Report, 1954.

(263) Eight Prerequisites to a Good Health Program. Departmental Paper, Department of Rural Sociology, 1954.

(264) The Future Population of North Carolina. Departmental Research Report, North Carolina Ag. Exp. Sta., 1954.

(265) On the Distinction Between Inverse Regression and Regression Indirectly Determined. Unpublished statistical paper, Department of Rural Sociology, 1954.

(266) A Note on "Bias and Error" in Multiple Choice Tests. An unpublished statistical paper in answer to Lyerly's note on "correcting for chance success in objective tests." Department of Rural Sociology, 1954.

(267) Medical Service Communities in North Carolina. Departmental Research Report, North Carolina Ag. Exp. Sta., 1954.

(268) Some Preliminary Reflections on the North Carolina Agricultural Challenge Program. Report to the Agricultural College Advisory Committee, 1954.

(269) (with Selz C. Mayo). Nowadays Tarheel Farmers Have More Book Larnin'. North Carolina Ag. Exp. Sta., *Research and Farming*, 8, Summer-Autumn 1954, Winter-Spring 1955.

(270) Improving Health Insurance in North Carolina. Prepared for the Subcommittee on Health Insurance, North Carolina Conference for Social Service, May 1955.

(271) A Statistical Model for the Analysis of the Effect of Birth Control and Sex Preference on the Sex Ratio by Number of Children per Family. Department of Rural Sociology Paper, June 1955.

(272) How Many of Our Farm Families Are Leaving the Farm? North Carolina Ag. Exp. Sta., *Research and Farming*, 14 (1 and 2), Summer-Autumn 1955.

(273) Insurance and Social Security for Farm People. Department of Rural Sociology Paper, 1955.

(274) (with Herbert A. Aurbach). Comparison of North Carolina with the United States and Other States on Selected Socioeconomic Variables. Report to the Director of the North Carolina Agricultural Experiment Station, December 1955.

(275) Raleigh School Census Plans: Schedules, Instructions, and Analysis, 1955.

(276) The Relation of Per Capita and Median Family Incomes to the Social and Economic Characteristics of the Population. Annual Report on Population Research Project, North Carolina State College, 1955.

(277) (with Herbert A. Aurbach) The Relationship of Income Measures to Population Factors and to Other Measures of Economic and Social Well-being. North Carolina State College, January 1956.

(278) What is Rural Sociology? Department of Rural Sociology Paper, North Carolina State College, January 1956.

(279) Community Development for Health: Rural and Agricultural Aspects. Address to the North Carolina Public Health Association meeting, May 1956.

(280) Analysis of a Single Dichotomous Distribution. Department of Rural Sociology Paper, North Carolina State College, October 1956.

(281) Who Spends What for Health in North Carolina? A Special Report prepared for a Committee of the North Carolina Health Council, October 1956.

(282) Rural Population and Per Capita Income. *The Progressive Farmer*, Raleigh, North Carolina, November 1956.

(283) Highlights of Rural Sociological Research, 1937-1955. Department of Rural Sociology Research Report, North Carolina State College, 1956.

(284) Important Organization Developments in Rural Sociology Since 1937. Department of Rural Sociology Paper, North Carolina State College, 1956.

(285) Net Migration from the Rural Farm Areas of North Carolina Counties During the Decade 1940 to 1950. Mimeographed Table, 1956.

(286) Net Migration Rates During the Decade 1940-1950 Among People 25-29 Years of Age in 1940 (or 35-39 in 1950) by Sex, Color, and Educational Level. United States Rural Farm, North Carolina Total and Rural Farm Populations. Department of Rural Sociology Research Paper, North Carolina State College, 1956.

(287) (with Selz C. Mayo) Population Characteristics and Trends in North Carolina. Dept. of Rural Sociology Research Report, North Carolina State College, 1956.

(288) The Relation of Per Capita and Median Family Incomes to the Social and Economic Characteristics of the Population. North Carolina Ag. Exp. Sta. Research Report, 1956.

(289) (as Chairman of a Committee) Report of the Committee on the 1960 United States Census. Rural Sociological Society, 10 pages, 1956.

(290) Retirement and Social Security: A Study of West Virginia's Teachers' Retirement System. *Time for Action,* Chapter 6, George Peabody College for Teachers, Nashville, Tenn., 1956.

(291) (with a Committee). What of Health Insurance? A Study of Health Insurance in North Carolina for the North Carolina Conference on Social Service, 1956.

(292) Increasing Enrollment of Voluntary Health Insurance in Low Income Areas Highlighted by Research Findings, and Wide Use Is Being Made of the Results of Rural Health Research. *Research Success Stories,* Dept. of Rural Sociology, North Carolina Ag. Exp. Sta., January 1957.

(293) Statistics on North Carolina Agriculture and Rural Farm Living: From the 1950 and 1954 United States Censuses of Agriculture. North Carolina Agricultural Extension Service, October 1957.

(294) Fall Enrollment in North Carolina State College with Projection to 1975. Dept. of Rural Sociology, North Carolina State College, December 1957.

(295) Long-Range Planning Report, Department of Rural Sociology, North Carolina State College, December 1957.

(296) Why Are We Low Income? North Carolina Ag. Exp. Sta., *Research and Farming,* 16(2): 10, 1957.

(297) Movement of Youth from Their Parental Homes, Montgomery and Stokes Counties, North Carolina, 1947-1956. Annual Report to North Carolina Experiment Station, February 1958.

(298) Analysis of the Public Welfare "A" Budget Requests in Terms of Expected Population Changes. Report for the North Carolina Department of the Budget, 1958.

(299) The Scholar in a Changing Society. Read to the annual meeting of the North Carolina State College Chapter of Phi Kappa Phi, April 1958. *Phi Kappa Phi Journal,* 37(3), 1958.

(300) Whither Our Youth? North Carolina Ag. Exp. Sta., *Research and Farming,* 16(4): 9, 1958.

(301) World Population Trends and Impact on Manpower Potential. (With data from United Nations Population Studies No. 28 and United States Bureau of the Census). Department of Rural Sociology Research Report, North Carolina Ag. Exp. Sta., 1958.

(302) (with J. Marshall Barber) How the State Can Save Its Employees and Taxpayers Over $4,000,000. Department of Rural Sociology, North Carolina State College, 1959.

Part II: Major Publications, 1966-1975

(303) Effect of Census Errors on the Measurement of Net Migration. *Demography*, 3(2): 393-415, 1966.

(304) (with R. David Mustian) Measuring the Extent, Character, and Direction of Occupational Change. *Social Forces*, 45(3): 440-444, January 1967.

(305) The Vital Statistics Method of Estimating Net Migration by Age Cohorts. *Demography*, 4(2): 464-487, 1967.

(306) The Need for Family Planning in North Carolina. UNC Newsletter, 53(3), September 1968.

(307) (with Theresa H. Ramsey) *Estimates of the Population of North Carolina Counties, 1967 and 1968—Components of Population Change Since 1960*. State Department of Administration, Statistical Services Center, Budget Division, and Chapel Hill, University of North Carolina, Carolina Population Center, Demographic Report H-2, April 1969, 19pp.

(308) (with Wen L. Li) Measuring the Need of Family Planning in North Carolina Counties. Abstracts of papers presented at the 32nd annual meeting of the Southern Sociological Society. *Sociological Abstracts* 17(2), Supl. 3, Part 2, 1969, 32 pp.

(309) (with Theresa H. Ramsey) *Estimates of the Population of North Carolina Counties, 1968 and 1969—Components of Population Change Since 1960*. State Department of Administration, Planning Division; and Chapel Hill, University of North Carolina, Carolina Population Center, Demographic Report H-3, March 1970, 19 pp.

(310) The USA South, its Changing Population Characteristics: A Graphic and Statistical Summary. Chapel Hill, University of North Carolina at Chapel Hill, Carolina Population Center, December 1970, 191 pp.

(311) Source Tables: Educational Selectivity of Net Internal Migration in the United States and its Four Major Regions During the Decade 1940-1950 by Age, Sex, and Color, Chapel Hill, North Carolina, Carolina Population Center, 1972, 71 pp.

(312) *North Carolina Population Trends: A Demographic Sourcebook*. Vol. 1-3, University of North Carolina, Carolina Population Center (for the Office of Station Planning), Chapel Hill, 1974-75, 125 pp. 212 pp. and 259 pp.

Appendix C
Conference Participants

Presenting Papers:

David L. Birch is Director of the Programs on Neighborhood and Regional Change at the Massachusetts Institute of Technology, Cambridge, Massachusetts.

Gladys K. Bowles was for many years a social demographer with the U.S. Department of Agriculture, specializing in studies of internal migration, rural population, and labor force. She retired from federal service in 1980, and is now the proprietor of Bowles Demographic Research in Athens, Georgia.

Peter K. Francese is Publisher of *American Demographics,* Ithaca, New York, a magazine which he founded in 1978. He is also a member of the Population Advisory Committee of the Bureau of the Census.

Harold F. Goldsmith is Associate Chief of the Mental Health Study Center, National Institute of Mental Health, Adelphi, Maryland.

Michael Greenberg is Professor of Environmental Planning and Geography at Rutgers University, New Brunswick, New Jersey.

Mary Kay Healy is currently the Manager of Demographics with Donnelley Marketing in Stanford, Connecticut. At the time of the conference, she was a statistical demographer in the Population Division of the Bureau of the Census.

David J. Jackson is Deputy Chief of the Population Research Section, Mental Health Study Center, National Institute of Mental Health, Adelphi, Maryland.

Everett S. Lee is Professor of Sociology at the University of Georgia, Athens, Georgia.

Peter A. Morrison is Director of the Population Research Center, the Rand Corporation, Santa Monica, California. His research interests include demographic forecasting and policy analysis related to U.S. population change. He has authored several publications dealing with population estimation and forecasting procedures.

Donald B. Pittenger is Director of the Demographic Laboratory, Olympia, Washington. At the time of the conference, he was Assistant Chief, Population Studies Division, Washington State, Office of Financial Management.

J. Philip Shambaugh is an Operations Research Analyst in the Department of Energy, Washington, D.C. At the time of the conference, he was a Social Science Analyst in the Population Research Section, Mental Health Study Center, National Institute of Mental Health, Adelphi, Maryland.

Norfleet W. Rives, Jr. is Associate Professor in the College of Urban Affairs and Public Policy and the Department of Mathematical Sciences at the University of Delaware. His major interest is the role of population estimates and projections in planning and public policy.

Other Participants:

Richard A. Engels, Assistant Chief of Population Estimation Projects, Population Division, Bureau of the Census, Suitland, Maryland.

Richard Irwin, Chief of Estimates Research Unit, Population Division, Bureau of the Census, Suitland, Maryland.

Anne S. Lee, Demographic Consultant, Athens, Georgia.

Beatrice M. Rosen, Chief, Evaluation and Need Assessment Section, Applied Biometrics Research Branch, Division of Biometry and Epidemiology, National Institute of Mental Health, Rockville, Maryland.

Harry M. Rosenberg, Chief of Mortality Statistics Branch, Division of Vital Statistics, National Center for Health Statistics, Hyattsville, Maryland.